Edward Sylvester Ellis

1000 MYTHOLOGICAL CHARACTERS BRIEFLY DESCRIBED

Table of contents

INTRODUCTION.

There are many expressions which, though simple in themselves, must forever remain beyond the grasp of human comprehension. Eternity, that which has neither end nor beginning, baffles the most profound human thought. It is impossible to think of a point beyond which there is absolutely nothing, or to imagine the passing of a million years without bringing us one day or one minute nearer to their close. Suppose that one could fix upon the terminal point, we would still fancy something beyond that, and then some period still more remote would present itself, and so on ad infinitum.

The same insurmountable difficulty confronts us when we seek to imagine a First Cause. God was the beginning, and yet it seems to our finite minds, that something must have brought Him into existence, and we conclude that back again of that creating Power must have been another originating cause, and perhaps still another, and so on without limitation.

And yet we know that there must have been a period when everything was void, or, in other words, when there was nothing. In the awful grandeur of that loneliness, desolation, and chaos, God we know, however, existed and called the universe into being. All that we, in our present finite condition, can ever comprehend of that stupendous birth is contained in the opening of the first chapter of Genesis.

That is the story of the creation as told by God Himself to His chosen people, the Hebrews, they alone being selected from the nations then existing upon the earth to receive the wonderful revelation.

Every people, no matter how degraded and sunken in barbarism, has some perception, some explanation of, and a more or less well-grounded belief in, a First Cause. Far back among the mists of antiquity, at the remotest beginnings of the shadowy centuries, sits enthroned a Being, who in His infinite

1

might and power brought mankind, the universe, and all animate and inanimate things into existence, and who rewards those of His children who do His will, and punishes those who disobey His commands. That will, as interpreted by believers, is as various in its application to the conduct of man as are the standards of right and wrong among the civilized and even among the barbarous nations of to-day. What is virtue with one is vice with the other, as beauty and ugliness of form or feature, being relative terms, are opposites with many different peoples.

Since the Greeks and Romans were not among those who received the divine story of creation, they were forced to devise a theory to explain their own existence and account for the origin of all things. The foundation of this theory lay in the marvelous phenomena of nature around them. The growth of the mighty tree from the tiny seed, the bursting bud and blossom, the changing hues and the fragrance of flowers, the alternation of day and night, the flash of the rock-rending lightning, the rage of the tempest, the flow of the rivers; the towering mountains, the lovely valleys; dew, rain, the clouds, and the ever-shifting panorama on every hand; the majestic sweep of the blazing worlds through space—all these pointed unerringly to a First Cause, which originally launched them into being, and maintains the constant order of things and the miraculous procession of the planets and the orderly succession of the seasons in obedience to laws that know no change.

To the Greeks and Romans, there was a time more remote than history gives us any account of, when there was neither land nor water, and when the earth and all things within and upon it were "without form and void." Over that misty, nebulous mixing and mingling brooded the god Chaos, who shared his throne with Nox, the goddess of night. From this union the innumerable myths gradually sprang up and developed, which in their own imaginative though often grotesque way explained the various phases of creation. These finally became crystallized into a literature, or mythology, which has since been the inspiration alike of romancers and poets.

The most learned of mythologists differ in their analysis of the multitude of myths that have descended to us. Their varying analyses, however, may be separated into two distinct classes or divisions, each of which has its own adherents and supporters.

The first school is that of the philologists, and the second that of the anthro-

pologists, or comparative mythologists.

Philology relates to the study of language, especially when treated in a philosophical manner. This school maintains that the myths had their origin in a "disease of the language, as the pearl is a result of a disease of the oyster." The key, therefore, to all mythologies, they say, is found in language. The names originally applied to the gods generally referred to the phenomena of the clouds, winds, rain, sunshine, etc. Latin, Greek, and Sanskrit, the great languages of antiquity, they demonstrate, had their foundation in a single source which is still older. As further proof of their position, they point to the similarity in the most ordinary words in the various languages of the same family, and show that they have undergone few or very trifling changes.

The greatest authority among the philologists claims that during the "first period" there was a tribe in Central Asia, whose language consisted of one-syllable words, which contained the germs of the Turanian, Aryan, and Semitic tongues. This age is termed the Rhematic period, and was succeeded by the Nomadic or Agglutinative age, during which the language gradually "received, once for all, that peculiar impress of their formative system which we still find in all the dialects and national idioms comprised under the name of Aryan or Semitic," which includes over three thousand dialects.

The same authority follows the Agglutinative period with one "represented everywhere by the same characteristic features, called the Mythological, or Mythopoeic age."

As the name implies, this last-mentioned period saw the evolution and development of mythic lore. As do the American Indians of to-day, so primitive man, in his crude way, explained the operation of physical laws by giving to inanimate objects like passions and sentiments with himself. When the tempest rages, and the crashing lightning splinters the mountain oak, the Indian says that the Great Spirit is angry. When nature becomes serene and calm, the Great Spirit is pleased. The malign forces around him, which work ill to the warrior, are, they say, the direct doings of an evil spirit. Even the heavenly bodies are personified, and "poetry has so far kept alive in our minds the old animative theory of nature, that it is no great effort in us to fancy the waterspout a huge giant or sea-monster, and to depict, in what we call appropriate metaphor, its march across the field of ocean."

Since the names of the Greek heroes and gods show a general correspondence with the Sanskrit appellations of physical things, it is comparatively easy to understand many of the first fancies and reflections of the earliest men who ever lived. It is the argument of the philologists that these fancies and reflections settled into definite shape in that far-away period when most of the nations, now spread to the remotest corners of the earth, dwelt together and used a common language. Following the gradual scattering of this single, unified people, the language became sensitive to the change, many words not only losing their original meaning, but, in some instances, acquiring an opposite significance. Other words, again, in the course of time were utterly lost. "As long as such personified beings as the Heaven or the Sun are consciously talked of in mythic language, the meaning of their legends is open to no question, and the action ascribed to them will, as a rule, be natural and appropriate." The time came, however, when these names were considered simply as applying to heroes or deities, and amid the jumble and confusion of the succeeding ages it became well-nigh impossible to trace the myths back to their original source and meaning. Such is a brief outline of the myth interpretations, as made by the philologists.

Anthropology may be defined as the study of man, considered in his entire nature. In explaining mythology, the anthropologists say that "it is man, it is human thought and human language combined, which naturally and necessarily produced the strange conglomerate of ancient fable." Instead, therefore, of seeking the source of myths in language, the second class find it in the "condition of thought through which all races have passed."

The argument of the anthropologists is that while all nations have come from one parent-stock, as is claimed also by the philologists, yet the various peoples, in their primitive or savage state, have passed through a like low intellectual condition and growth. The folk-lore of all countries shows that the savages consider themselves of the same nature as beasts, and regard "even plants, inanimate objects, and the most abstract phenomena as persons with human parts and passions." Every religion antedating Christianity has inculcated the worship of idols, which usually take the form of beasts, and it will be noted in the study of myths that the gods often assume the forms of birds and animals. If it were in our power mentally to become savages for a time, so as to look upon nature and our surroundings as do the Blackfeet In-

dians, or the Patagonians, or the South Africans, it would be a long step toward making clear this particular phase of the question.

From what has been stated, however, the young student will gain an idea of the meaning of the word "myth," which may be termed a story whose origin can never be known with certainty. To most people it has the same significance as a fable, legendary tale, or fanciful falsehood. A collection of myths belonging to a particular age or people is "a mythology," and the branch of inquiry which classifies and interprets them bears the same name.

THE YOUTH'S DICTIONARY
OF MYTHOLOGY.

Abas (A'bas), a son of Meganira, was turned into a newt, or water-lizard, for deriding the ceremonies of the Sacrifice.

Absyrtus (Absy'rtus). After Jason had slain the dragon which guarded the golden fleece, he fled with Medea, the beautiful young sorceress, and daughter of Aeetes, who pursued with great energy, for Medea had taken with her the most precious treasure of the king, his only son and heir, Absyrtus. To delay the pursuit, Medea slew her little brother, cut the body in pieces, and dropped them over the side of the vessel. Thus the cruel daughter effected her escape.

Achelous (Achelo'us) was a river god, and the rival of Hercules in his love for Deianira. To decide who should have the bride, Hercules and Achelous had recourse to a wrestling bout, the fame of which extends through all the intervening centuries. In this fierce struggle, Achelous changed himself into the form of a bull and rushed upon his antagonist with lowered horns, intending to hurl him aside. Hercules eluded the onset, and seizing one of the huge horns, held it so firmly that it was broken off by the furious efforts of Achelous to free himself. He was defeated, and finally turned himself into a river, which has since been known by his name.

Acheron (Ach'eron) (see "The Youth's Classical Dictionary"). The current of the river Acheron, across which all souls had to pass to

hear their decree from Pluto, was so swift that the boldest swimmer
dare not attempt to breast it; and, since there was no bridge, the spirits were obliged to rely upon the aid of Charon, an aged boatman,
who plied the only boat that was available. He would allow no soul to
enter this leaky craft until he had received the obolus, or fare, which
the ancients carefully placed under the tongue of the dead, that they
might not be delayed in their passage to Pluto. Those who had not
their fare were forced to wait one hundred years, when Charon re-
luctantly ferried them over without charge.

"Infernal rivers that disgorge
Into the burning lake their baleful streams
... Sad Acheron, of sorrow black and deep."
Milton.

Achilles (Achil'les) was the most valiant of the Greek heroes in the
Trojan War. He was the son of Peleus, King of Thessaly. His mother,
Thetis, plunged him, when an infant, into the Stygian pool, which
made him invulnerable wherever the waters had washed him; but
the heel by which he was held was not wetted, and that part remained vulnerable. He was shot with an arrow in the heel by Paris, at the
siege of Troy, and died of his wound.
Acidalia (Acida'lia), a name given to Venus, from a fountain in Boeotia.
Acis (A'cis). A Sicilian shepherd, loved by the nymph Galatea. One of
the Cyclops who was jealous of him crushed him by hurling a rock
on him. Galatea turned his blood into a river—the Acis at the foot of
Mount Etna.
Actaeon (Actae'on) was the son of Aristaeus, a famous huntsman. He
intruded himself on Diana while she was bathing, and was changed
by her into a deer, in which form he was hunted by his own dogs
and torn in pieces.
Ades (A'des), see Hades.

Adonis (Ado′nis), the beautiful attendant of Venus, who held her train. He was killed by a boar, and turned by Venus into an anemone.

"Even as the sun with purple-colored face
Had ta'en his last leave of the weeping morn.
Rose-cheeked Adonis hied him to the chase;
Hunting he loved, but love he laughed to scorn."
Shakespeare.

Adrastaea (Adrastae′a), another name of Nemesis, one of the goddesses of justice.
Adscriptitii Dii (Adscripti′tii Dii) were the gods of the second grade.
Adversity, see Echidna.
Aeacus (Ae′acus), one of the judges of hell, with Minos and Rhadamanthus. See Eacus.
Aecastor (Aecas′tor), an oath used only by women, referring to the Temple of Castor.
Aedepol (Aed′epol), an oath used by both men and women, referring to the Temple of Pollux.
Aeetes (Aee′tes), a king of Colchis, and father of Medea.
Aegeon (Aege′on), a giant with fifty heads and one hundred hands, who was imprisoned by Jupiter under Mount Etna. See Briareus.
Aegis (Ae′gis), the shield of Jupiter, so called because it was made of goat-skin.

"Where was thine Aegis Pallas that appall'd?"
Byron.

"Tremendous, Gorgon frowned upon its field,

And circling terrors filled the expressive shield."

"Full on the crest the Gorgon's head they place,
With eyes that roll in death, and with distorted face."
Pope.

Aegle (Ae′gle). The fairest of the Naiads.
Aello (Ael′lo), the name of one of the Harpies.
Aeneas (Aene′as) was the son of Anchises and Venus. He was one of
the few great captains who escaped the destruction of Troy. He be-
haved with great valor during the siege, encountering Diomed, and
even Achilles himself. When the Grecians had set the city on fire Aeneas took his aged father, Anchises, on his shoulders, while his son,
Ascanius, and his wife Creusa, clung to his garments. He saved them
all from the flames. After wandering about during several years, encountering numerous difficulties, he at length arrived in Italy, where
he was hospitably received by Latinus, king of the Latins. After the
death of Latinus Aeneas became king.

"His back, or rather burthen, showed
As if it stooped with its load;
For as Aeneas bore his sire
Upon his shoulders through the fire,
Our knight did bear no less a pack
Of his own buttocks on his back."
Butler.

Aeolus (Aeo′lus) was the god of the winds. Jupiter was his reputed father, and his mother is said to have been a daughter of Hippotus.

Aeolus is represented as having the power of holding the winds confined in a cavern, and occasionally giving them liberty to blow over the world. So much command was he supposed to have over them that when Ulysses visited him on his return from Troy he gave him, tied up in a bag, all the winds that could prevent his voyage from being prosperous. The companions of Ulysses, fancying that the bag contained treasure, cut it open just as they came in sight of Ithaca, the port they were making for, and the contrary winds rushing out drove back the ship many leagues. The residence of Aeolus was at Strongyle, now called Strombolo.

"Aeolus from his airy throne
With power imperial curbs the struggling winds,
And sounding tempests in dark prisons binds."
Dryden.

Aesculapius (Aescula'pius), the god of physic, was a son of Apollo. He was physician to the Argonauts in their famous expedition to Colchis. He became so noted for his cures that Pluto became jealous of him, and he requested Jupiter to kill him with a thunderbolt. To revenge his son's death Apollo slew the Cyclops who had forged the thunderbolt. By his marriage with Epione he had two sons, Machaon and Podalirius, both famous physicians, and four daughters, of whom Hygeia, the goddess of health, is the most renowned. Many temples were erected in honor of Aesculapius, and votive tablets were hung therein by people who had been healed by him; but his most famous shrine was at Epidaurus, where, every five years, games were held in his honor. This god is variously represented, but the most famous statue shows him seated on a throne of gold and ivory. His head is crowned with rays, and he wears a long beard. A knotty stick is in one hand, and a staff entwined with a serpent is in the other, while a dog lies at his feet.

"Thou that dost Aesculapius deride,
And o'er his gallipots in triumph ride."
Fenton.

Aeson (Ae'son) was father of Jason, and was restored to youth by Medea.

Agamemnon (Agamem'non) was the son of Plisthenes and brother of Menelaus. He was king of the Argives. His brother's wife was the famous Helen, daughter of Tyndarus, king of Sparta; and when she eloped with Paris, Agamemnon was appointed leader of the Greeks in their expedition against Troy.

Aganippides (Aganip'pides), a name of the Muses, derived from the fountain of Aganippe.

Agineus (Agine'us), see Apollo.

Aglaia (Agla'ia) was one of the Three Graces.

Agni (Ag'ni). The Hindoo god of lightning.

Ajax (A'jax) was one of the bravest of the Greek warriors in the Trojan War. His father was Telamon, and his mother Eriboea. Some writers say that he was killed by Ulysses; others aver that he was slain by Paris; while others again assert that he went mad after being defeated by Ulysses, and killed himself. Another Ajax, son of Oileus, also took a prominent part in the Trojan War.

Alcestis (Alces'tis), wife of Admetus, who, to save her husband's life, died in his stead, and was restored to life by Hercules.

Alcides (Alci'des), one of the names of Hercules.

Alcmena (Alcme'na), the mother of Hercules, was daughter of Electryon, a king of Argos.

Alecto (Alec'to) was one of the Furies. She is depicted as having serpents instead of hair on her head, and was supposed to breed pestilence wherever she went.

Alectryon (Alec'tryon), a servant of Mars, who was changed by him into a cock because he did not warn his master of the rising of the sun.

Alfadur (Al'fadur), in Scandinavian Mythology the Supreme Being—
Father of all.

Alma Mammosa (Al'ma Mammo'sa), a name of Ceres.

Alpheus (Alphe'us), a river god. See Arethusa.

Altar. A structure on which a sacrifice was offered. The earliest altars
were merely heaps of earth or turf or rough unhewn stone; but as
the mode of sacrificing became more ceremonious grander altars
were built. Some were of marble and brass, ornamented with car-
vings and bas-reliefs, and the corners with models of the heads of
animals. They varied in height from two feet to twenty, and some
were built solid; others were made hollow to retain the blood of the
victims. Some were provided with a kind of dish, into which frankincense was thrown to overpower the smell of burning fat. This proba-
bly was the origin of the custom of burning incense at the altar.

Amalthaea (Amal'thae'a), the goat which nourished Jupiter.

Amazons (Am'azons) were a nation of women-soldiers who lived in
Scythia. Hercules totally defeated them, and gave Hippolyte, their
queen, to Theseus for a wife. The race seems to have been extermi-
nated after this battle.

Amazon

Ambarvalia (Ambarva′lia) were festivals in honor of Ceres, instituted by Roman husbandmen to purge their fields. At the spring festival the head of each family led an animal, usually a pig or ram, decked with oak boughs, round his grounds, and offered milk and new wine. After harvest there was another festival, at which Ceres was presented with the first-fruits of the season. See Ceres.

Amber, see Heliades.

Ambrosia (Ambro′sia) were Bacchanalian festivals.

Amica (Ami′ca), a name of Venus.

Amphion (Amphi′on) was the son of Jupiter and Antiope. He was greatly skilled in music; and it is said that, at the sound of his lute, the stones arranged themselves so regularly as to make the walls of the city of Thebes.

"Amphion, too, as story goes, could call

Obedient stones to make the Theban wall."
Horace.

"New walls to Thebes, Amphion thus began."
William King.

"Such strains I sing as once Amphion played,
When list'ning flocks the powerful call obeyed."
Elphinston.

Amphitrite (Amphitri′te) (or Salatia), the wife of Neptune, was a daughter of Oceanus and Tethys. She was the mother of Triton, a sea god.
"His weary chariot sought the bowers
Of Amphitrite and her tending nymphs."
Thomson.

Amycus (Amy′cus) was king of Bebrycia. He was a son of Neptune, and was killed by Pollux.
Ancaeus (Ancae′us). A son of Neptune, who left a cup of wine to hunt a wild boar which killed him, and the wine was untasted. This was the origin of the proverb—"There's many a slip 'twixt cup and lip."
Ancilia (Ancil′ia), the twelve sacred shields. The first Ancile was supposed to have fallen from heaven in answer to the prayer of Numa Pompilius. It was kept with the greatest care, as it was prophesied that the fate of the Roman people would depend upon its preservation. An order of priesthood was established to take care of the Anci-

lia, and on 1st March each year the shields were carried in procession, and in the evening there was a great feast, called Coena Saliaris.

Andromeda (Androm′eda), the daughter of Cepheus, king of the Ethiopians, was wife of Perseus, by whom she was rescued when she was chained to a rock and was about to be devoured by a sea-monster.

Anemone (Anem′one). Venus changed Adonis into this flower.

Angeronia (Angero′nia), otherwise Volupia, was the goddess who had the power of dispelling anguish of mind.

Anna Perenna (Anna Peren′na), one of the rural divinities.

Antaeus (Antae′us), a giant who was vanquished by Hercules. Each time that Hercules threw him the giant gained fresh strength from touching the earth, so Hercules lifted him off the ground and squeezed him to death.

Anteros (An′teros), one of the two Cupids, sons of Venus.

Anticlea (Antic′lea), the mother of Ulysses.

Antiope (Anti′ope) was the wife of Lycus, King of Thebes. Jupiter, disguised as a satyr, led her astray and corrupted her.

Anubis (Anu′bis) (or Hermanubis (Herman′ubis)). "A god half a dog, a dog half a man." Called Barker by Virgil and other poets.

Aonides (Aon′ides), a name of the Muses, from the country Aonia.

Apaturia (Apatur′ia), an Athenian festival, which received its name from a Greek word signifying deceit.

Aphrodite (Aph′rodi′te), a Greek name of Venus.

Apis, a name given to Jupiter by the inhabitants of the Lower Nile. Also the miraculous ox, worshiped in Egypt.

Apis (A′pis), King of Argivia. Afterward called Serapis, the greatest god of the Egyptians.

Apollo (Apol′lo). This famous god, some time King of Arcadia, was the son of Jupiter and Latona. He was known by several names, but principally by the following:—Sol (the sun); Cynthius, from the mountain called Cynthus in the Isle of Delos, and this same island being his native place obtained for him the name of Delius; Delphinius, from his occasionally assuming the shape of a dolphin. His name of Delphicus was derived from his connection with the splendid Temple at Delphi, where he uttered the famous oracles. Some writers record that this oracle became dumb when Jesus Christ was born. Other common names of Apollo were Didymaeus, Nomius, Paean, and Phoebus. The Greeks called him Agineus, because the streets were under his guardianship, and he was called Pythius from having killed the serpent Python. Apollo is usually represented as a handsome young man without beard, crowned with laurel, and having in one hand a bow, and in the other a lyre. The favorite residence of Apollo was on Mount Parnassus, a mountain of Phocis, in Greece, where he presided over the Muses. Apollo was the accredited father of several children, but the two most renowned were Aesculapius and Phaeton.

"Wilt thou have music? Hark! Apollo plays.
And twenty cagëd nightingales do sing."
Shakespeare.

Apotheosis (Apothe'osis). The consecration of a god. The ceremony of deification.

Arachne (Arach'ne), a Lydian princess, who challenged Minerva to a spinning contest, but Minerva struck her on the head with a spindle, and turned her into a spider.

"... So her disemboweled web,
Arachne, in a hall or kitchen spreads.
Obvious to vagrant flies."
John Phillips.

Arcadia (Arca'dia), a delightful country in the center of Peloponnessus, a favorite place of the gods. Apollo was reputed to have been King of Arcadia.

Arcas (Ar'cas), a son of Calisto, was turned into a he-bear; and afterward into the constellation called Ursa Minor.

Archer, see Chiron.

Areopagitae (Areop′agi′tae), the judges who sat at the Areopagus.

Areopagus (Areop′agus), the hill at Athens where Mars was tried for murder before twelve of the gods.

Ares (A′res). The same as Mars, the god of war.

Arethusa (Arethu′sa) was one of the nymphs of Diana. She fled from Alpheus, a river god, and was enabled to escape by being turned by Diana into a rivulet which ran underground. She was as virtuous as she was beautiful.

Argonauts (Ar′gonauts). This name was given to the fifty heroes who sailed to Colchis in the ship Argo, under the command of Jason, to fetch the Golden Fleece.

Argus (Ar′gus) was a god who had a hundred eyes which slept and watched by turns. He was charged by Juno to watch Io, but, being slain by Mercury, was changed by Juno into a peacock.

Ariadne (Ariad′ne), daughter of Minos, King of Crete. After enabling Theseus to get out of the Labyrinth by means of a clew of thread, she fled with him to Naxos, where he ungratefully deserted her; but Bacchus wooed her and married her, and the crown of seven stars which he gave her was turned into a constellation.

Arion (Ari′on) was a famous lyric poet of Methymna, in the Island of Lesbos, where he gained great riches by his art. There is a pretty fable which has made the name of Arion famous. Once when traveling from Lesbos his companions robbed him, and proposed to throw him into the sea. He entreated the seamen to let him play upon his harp before they threw him overboard, and he played so sweetly that the dolphins flocked round the vessel. He then threw himself into the sea, and one of the dolphins took him up and carried him to Taenarus, near Corinth. For this act the dolphin was raised to heaven as a constellation.

Aristaeus (Aristae′us), son of Apollo and Cyrene, was the god of trees; he also taught mankind the use of honey, and how to get oil from olives. He was a celebrated hunter. His most famous son was

Actaeon.

Armata (Arma′ta), one of the names of Venus, given to her by Spartan women.

Artemis (Ar′temis). This was the Grecian name of Diana, and the festivals at Delphi were called Artemisia.

Arts and Sciences, see Muses.

Aruspices (Arus′pices), sacrificial priests.

Ascalaphus (Ascal′aphus) was changed into an owl, the harbinger of misfortune, by Ceres, because he informed Pluto that Proserpine had partaken of food in the infernal regions, and thus prevented her return to earth.

Ascanius (Asca′nius), the son of Aeneas and Creusa.

Ascolia (Ascol′ia), Bacchanalian feasts, from a Greek word meaning a leather bottle. The bottles were used in the games to jump on.

Asopus (Aso′pus). A son of Jupiter, who was killed by one of his father's thunderbolts.

Assabinus (Assabi′nus), the Ethiopian name of Jupiter.

Ass's ears, see Midas.

Astarte (Astar′te), one of the Eastern names of Venus.

Asteria (Aste′ria), daughter of Caeus, was carried away by Jupiter, who assumed the shape of an eagle.

Astrea (Astre′a), mother of Nemesis, was the goddess of justice; she returned to heaven when the earth became corrupt.

"... Chaste Astrea fled,
And sought protection in her native sky."
John Hughes.

Atalanta (Atalan′ta) was daughter of Caeneus. The oracle told her that marriage would be fatal to her, but, being very beautiful, she had many suitors. She was a very swift runner, and, to get rid of her admirers, she promised to marry any one of them who should ou-tstrip her in a race, but that all who were defeated should be slain. Hippomenes, however, with the aid of Venus, was successful. That goddess gave him three golden apples, one of which he dropped whenever Atalanta caught up to him in the race. She stopped to pick them up, and he was victorious and married her. They were both af-terward turned into lions by Cybele, for profaning her temple.

Ate (A'te). The goddess of revenge, also called the goddess of discord and all evil. She was banished from heaven by her father Jupiter.

"With Ate by his side come hot from hell."
Shakespeare.

Athena (Athe'na), a name obtained by Minerva as the tutelary god-dess of Athens.

Atlas, was King of Mauritania, now Morocco, in Africa. He was also a great astronomer. He is depicted with the globe on his back, his name signifying great toil or labor. For his inhospitality to Perseus that king changed him into the mountain which bears his name of Atlas. A chain of mountains in Africa is called after him, and so is the Atlantic Ocean. He had seven daughters by his wife Pleione, they were called by one common name, Pleiades; and by his wife Aethra he had seven more, who were, in the same manner, called Hyades. Both the Pleiades and the Hyades are celestial constellations.

Atreus (At'reus), the type of fraternal hatred. His dislike of his bro-ther Thyestes went to the extent of killing and roasting his nephews, and inviting their father to a feast, which Thyestes thought was a sign of reconciliation, but he was the victim of his brother's detesta-ble cruelty.

"Media must not draw her murdering knife,
Nor Atreus there his horrid feast prepare."
Lord Roscommon.

Atropos (At´ropos), one of the three sisters called The Fates, who held the shears ready to cut the thread of life.

Atys (A´tys), son of Croesus, was born dumb, but when in a fight he saw a soldier about to kill the king he gained speech, and cried out, "Save the king!" and the string that held his tongue was broken.

Atys (A´tys) was a youth beloved by Aurora, and was slain by her father, but, according to Ovid, was afterward turned into a pine-tree.

Augaeas (Aug´aeas), a king of Elis, the owner of the stable which Hercules cleansed after three thousand oxen had been kept in it for thirty years. It was cleansed by turning the river Alpheus through it. Augaeas promised to give Hercules a tenth part of his cattle for his trouble but, for neglecting to keep his promise, Hercules slew him.

Augury (Au´gury). This was a means adopted by the Romans of forming a judgment of futurity by the flight of birds, and the officiating priest was called an augur.

Aurora (Auro´ra), the goddess of the morning,

"Whose rosy fingers ope the gates of day."

She was daughter of Sol, the sun, and was the mother of the stars and winds. She is represented as riding in a splendid golden chariot drawn by white horses. The goddess loved Tithonus, and begged the gods to grant him immortality, but forgot to ask at the same time that he should not get old and decrepit. See Tithonus.

"... So soon as the all-cheering sun
Should, in the farthest east, begin to draw
The shady curtains of Aurora's bed."
Shakespeare.

Auster (Aus´ter), the south wind, a son of Jupiter.

Avernus (Aver'nus), a poisonous lake, referred to by poets as being at the entrance of the infernal regions, but it was really a lake in Campania, in Italy.

Averruncus Deus (Averrun'cus Deus), a Roman god, who could divert people from evil-doing.

Axe, see Daedalus.

Baal (Ba'al), a god of the Phoenicians.

Baal-Peor (Ba'al-Pe'or), a Moabitish god, associated with licentiousness and obscenity. The modern name is Belphegor.

Babes, see Rumia Dea.

Bacchantes (Bac'chantes). The priestesses of Bacchus.

Bacchus (Bac'chus), the god of wine, was the son of Jupiter and Semele. He is said to have married Ariadne, daughter of Minos, King of Crete, after she was deserted by Theseus. The most distinguished of his children is Hymen, the god of marriage. Bacchus is sometimes referred to under the names of Dionysius, Biformis, Brisaeus, Iacchus, Lenaeus, Lyceus, Liber, and Liber Pater, the symbol of liberty. The god of wine is usually represented as crowned with vine and ivy leaves. In his left hand is a thyrsus, a kind of javelin, having a fir cone for the head, and being encircled with ivy or vine. His chariot is drawn by lions, tigers, or panthers.

"Jolly Bacchus, god of pleasure,
Charmed the world with drink and dances."
T. Parnell, 1700.

Balios (Ba'lios). A famous horse given by Neptune to Peleus as a wedding present, and was afterward given to Achilles.

Barker, see Anubis.

Bassarides (Bassar'ides). The priestesses of Bacchus were sometimes so called.

Battle, see Valhalla.

Bear, see Calisto.

Beauty, see Venus.

Bees, see Mellona.

Belisama (Belisa′ma), a goddess of the Gauls. The name means the Queen of Heaven.

Bellerophon (Beller′ophon), a hero who destroyed a monster called the Chimaera.

Bellona (Bello′na), the goddess of war, and wife of Mars. The 24th March was called Bellona's Day, when her votaries cut themselves with knives and drank the blood of the sacrifice.

"In Dirae's and in Discord's steps Bellona treads,
And shakes her iron rod above their heads."

Belphegor (Belphe′gor), see Baal-Peor.

Belus (Be′lus). The Chaldean name of the sun.

Berecynthia (Berecyn′thia), a name of Cybele, from a mountain where she was worshiped.

Biformis (Bi′formis), a name of Bacchus, because he was accounted both bearded and beardless.

Birds, see Augury.

Births, see Lucina and Levana.

Blacksmith, see Brontes and Vulcan.

Blind, see Thamyris.

Blue eyes, see Glaukopis.

Bona Dea (Bo′na De′a). "The bountiful goddess," whose festival was celebrated by the Romans with much magnificence. See Ceres.

Bonus Eventus (Bo′nus Even′tus). The god of good success, a rural divinity.

Boreas (Bo′reas), the north wind, son of Astraeus and Aurora.

"... I snatched her from the rigid north,
Her native bed, on which bleak Boreas blew,
And bore her nearer to the sun...."
Young, 1710.

Boundaries, see Terminus.

Boxing, see Pollux.

Brahma (Brah'ma). The great Indian deity, represented with four heads looking to the four quarters of the globe.

Briareus (Bri'areus), a famous giant. See Aegeon.

Brisaeus (Bris'aeus). A name of Bacchus, referring to the use of grapes and honey.

Brontes (Bront'es), one of the Cyclops. He is the personification of a blacksmith.

Bubona (Bubo'na), goddess of herdsmen, one of the rural divinities.

Buddha (Bud'dha). Primitively, a pagan deity, the Vishnu of the Hindoos.

Byblis (Byb'lis). A niece of Sol, mentioned by Ovid. She shed so many tears for unrequited love that she was turned into a fountain.
"Thus the Phoebeian Byblis, spent in tears,
Becomes a living fountain, which yet bears
Her name."
Ovid.

Cabiri (Cab'iri). The mysterious rites connected with the worship of these deities were so obscene that most writers refer to them as secrets which it was unlawful to reveal.

Cacodaemon (Cac'odae'mon). The Greek name of an evil spirit.

Cacus (Ca'cus), a three-headed monster and robber.

Cadmus (Cad'mus), one of the earliest of the Greek demi-gods. He was the reputed inventor of letters, and his alphabet consisted of sixteen letters. It was Cadmus who slew the Boeotian dragon, and sowed its teeth in the ground, from each of which sprang up an armed man.

Caduceus (Cadu'ceus). The rod carried by Mercury. It has two winged serpents entwined round the top end. It was supposed to possess the power of producing sleep, and Milton refers to it in Paradise Lost as the "opiate rod."

Calisto (Calis'to), an Arcadian nymph, who was turned into a she-bear by Jupiter. In that form she was hunted by her son Arcas, who would have killed her had not Jupiter turned him into a he-bear. The nymph and her son form the constellations known as the Great Bear and Little Bear.

Calliope (Calli'ope). The Muse who presided over epic poetry and rhetoric. She is generally depicted using a stylus and wax tablets, the ancient writing materials.

Calpe (Cal'pe). One of the pillars of Hercules.

Calypso (Calyp'so) was queen of the island of Ogygia, on which Ulysses was wrecked, and where he was persuaded to remain seven years.

Cama (Ca'ma). The Indian god of love and marriage.

Camillus (Camil'lus), a name of Mercury, from his office of minister to the gods.

Canache (Can'ache). The name of one of Actaeon's hounds.

Canopus (Cano'pus). The Egyptian god of water, the conqueror of fire.

Capis (Cap'is) or Capula (Cap'ula). A peculiar cup with ears, used in drinking the health of the deities.

Capitolinus (Capitoli'nus). A name of Jupiter, from the Capitoline hill, on the top of which a temple was built and dedicated to him.

Capripedes (Cap'ri'pedes). Pan, the Egipans, the Satyrs, and Fauns, were so called from having goat's feet.

Caprotina (Caproti'na). A name of Juno.

Cassandra (Cassan'dra), a daughter of Priam and Hecuba, who was granted by Apollo the power of seeing into futurity, but having offended that god he prevented people from believing her predictions.

Cassiopeia (Cassiope'ia). The Ethiopian queen who set her beauty in comparison with that of the Nereides, who thereupon chained her to a rock and left her to be devoured by a sea-monster, but she was delivered by Perseus. See Andromeda.

Castalia (Casta′lia). One of the fountains in Mount Parnassus, sacred to the Muses.

Castalides (Casta′li′des), a name of the Muses, from the fountain Castalia or Castalius.

Castor (Cas′tor), son of Jupiter and Leda, twin brother of Pollux, noted for his skill in horsemanship. He went with Jason in quest of the Golden Fleece.

Cauther (Cau′ther), in Mohammedan mythology, is the lake of paradise, whose waters are as sweet as honey, as cold as snow, and as clear as crystal; and any believer who tastes thereof is said to thirst no more.

Celeno (Cel′eno) was one of the Harpies, progenitor of Zephyrus, the west wind.

Centaur (Cen′taur). A huntsman who had the forepart like a man, and the remainder of the body like a horse. The Centauri lived in Thessaly.

Cephalus (Cep′halus) was married to Procris, whom he accidentally slew by shooting her while she was secretly watching him, he thinking she was a wild beast. Cephalus was the type of constancy.

Ceraunius (Cerau′nius). A Greek name of Jupiter, meaning The Fulminator, from his thunderbolts.

Cerberus (Cer′berus). Pluto's famous three-headed dog, which guarded the gate of the infernal regions, preventing the living from entering, and the inhabitants from going out.

"Three-headed Cerberus, by fate
Posted at Pluto's iron gate;
Low crouching rolls his haggard eyes,
Ecstatic, and foregoes his prize."

Ceremonies, see Themis.

See page <u>23</u>
Apollo Belvedere
Ceres (Ce′res), daughter of Saturn, the goddess of agriculture, and of the fruits of the earth. She taught Triptolemus how to grow corn, and sent him to teach the inhabitants of the earth. She was known by the names of Magna Dea, Bona Dea, Alma Mammosa, and Thesmorphonis. Ceres was the mother of Proserpine. See Ambarvalia.
"To Ceres bland, her annual rites be paid
On the green turf beneath the fragrant shade.—
... Let all the hinds bend low at Ceres' shrine,
Mix honey sweet for her with milk and mellow wine,
Thrice lead the victim the new fruits around,
On Ceres call, and choral hymns resound."

"Ceres was she who first our furrows plowed,
Who gave sweet fruits and every good allowed."
Pope.

Cestus (Ces′tus), the girdle of Venus, which excited irresistible affection.
Chaos (Cha′os) allegorically represented the confused mass of matter supposed to have existed before the creation of the world, and out of which the world was formed.
"... Behold the throne
Of Chaos, and his dark pavilion spread
Wide on the wasteful deep; with him enthroned
Sat sable-vested Night, eldest of all things,
The consort of his reign."
Milton.

Charon (Char′on) was the son of Nox and Erebus. He was the ferryman who conveyed the spirits of the dead, in a boat, over the rivers Acheron and Styx to the Elysian Fields. "Charon's toll" was a coin put into the hands of the dead with which to pay the grim ferryman.
"From the dark mansions of the dead,
Where Charon with his lazy boat
Ferries o'er Lethe's sedgy moat."

Charybdis (Charyb′dis). A dangerous whirlpool on the coast of Sicily. Personified, it was supposed to have been a woman who plundered travelers, but was at last killed by Hercules. Scylla and Charybdis are generally spoken of together to represent alternative dangers.
"Charybdis barks, and Polyphemus roars."

Francis.

Chemos (Che′mos). The Moabitish god of war.
Children, see Nundina.
Chimaera (Chimae′ra). A wild illusion, personified in the monster slain by Bellerophon. It had the head and breast of a lion, the body of a goat, and the tail of a serpent. It used to vomit fire.
"... And on the craggy top
Chimera dwells, with lion's face and mane,
A goat's rough body and a serpent's train."
Pope.

"First, dire Chimera's conquest was enjoined,
A mingled monster of no mortal kind.
Behind, a dragon's fiery tail was spread,
A goat's rough body bore a lion's head,
Her pitchy nostrils flaky flames expire,
Her gaping throat emits infernal fire."
Milton.

Chiron (Chi′ron), the centaur who taught Achilles hunting, music, and the use of medicinal herbs. Jupiter placed him among the stars, where he appears as Sagittarius, the Archer.
Chloris (Chlo′ris). The Greek name of Flora, the goddess of flowers.
Chou. An Egyptian god corresponding to the Roman Hercules.
Chronos (Chro′nos). Time, the Grecian name of Saturn.
Cillaros (Cil′laros), see Cyllaros.
Circe (Cir′ce), daughter of the Sun. The knowledge of poisonous

herbs enabled her to destroy her husband, the King of the Sarmatians, for which act she was banished. When Ulysses landed at Aeaea, where she lived, she turned all his followers into swine.

Cisseta (Cisse'ta). The name of one of Actaeon's hounds.

Citherides (Cither'ides). A name of the Muses, from Mount Citheron.

Clio (Cli'o). One of the Muses, daughter of Jupiter and Mnemosyne. She presided over history.

Cloacina (Cloaci'na). The Roman goddess of sewers.

Clotho (Clo'tho) was one of the Fates. She was present at births, and held the distaff from which was spun the thread of life. See Atropos and Lachesis.

Clowns of Lycia, The (Ly'cia), were changed into frogs by Latona, because they refused to allow her to drink at one of their streamlets.

Cluacina (Clu'aci'na). A name of Venus, given to her at the time of the reconciliation of the Romans and the Sabines, which was ratified near a statue of the goddess.

Clytemnestra (Cly'temnes'tra), wife of Agamemnon, slew her husband and married Aegisthus. She attempted to kill her son Orestes, but he was delivered by his sister Electra, who sent him away to Strophius. He afterward returned and slew both Clytemnestra and Aegisthus.

Clytie (Clyt'ie). A nymph who got herself changed into a sunflower because her love of Apollo was unrequited. In the form of this flower she is still supposed to be turning toward Sol, a name of Apollo.

Cneph. In Egyptian mythology the creator of the universe.

Cocytus (Cocy'tus), the river of Lamentation. One of the five rivers of the infernal regions.

"Infernal rivers that disgorge
Into the burning lake their baleful streams.
... Cocytus, named of lamentation loud.
Heard on the rueful stream."
Milton.

Coeculus (Coe'culus), a violent robber, was a son of Vulcan.

Coelus (Coe'lus), also called Uranus (or Heaven), was the most ancient of the gods.

Coena Saliaris (Coe'na Salia'ris), see Ancilia.

Collina (Colli'na) was one of the rural deities, the goddess of hills.

Comedy, see Thalia.

Comus (Co'mus) was the god of revelry. He presided over entertainments and feasts.

Concord (Con'cord). The symbol of Concord was two right hands joined, and a pomegranate.

Concordia (Concor'dia). The goddess of peace. One of the oldest Roman goddesses. She is represented as holding a horn of plenty in one hand, and in the other a scepter, from which fruit is sprouting forth.

Constancy, see Cephalus.

Consualia (Consu'alia). Games sacred to Neptune.

Consus (Con'sus). A name given to Neptune as being the god of counsel.

Cophetua (Cophe'tua). A legendary king of Africa, who disliked women, but ultimately fell in love with a "beggar-maid," as mentioned in Romeo and Juliet.

"... Cupid, he that shot so trim
When King Cophetua loved the beggar-maid."
Shakespeare.

Copia (Co'pia), the goddess of plenty.

Coran (Co'ran). One of Actaeon's hounds was so named.

Corn, see Ceres.

Coronis (Cor'onis), was a consort of Apollo and mother of Aesculapius. Another Coronis was daughter of a king of Phocis, and was changed by Athena into a crow.

Corybantes (Coryban′tes) were priests of Cybele. They obtained the name because they were in the habit of striking themselves in their dances.

Corydon (Cory′don). A silly love-sick swain mentioned by Virgil.

Corythaix (Cory′thaix). A name given to Mars, meaning Shaker of the Helmet.

Cotytto (Cotyt′to). The Athenian goddess of immodesty.

"Hail! goddess of nocturnal sport,
Dark-veiled Cotytto, to whom the secret flame
Of midnight torches burns; mysterious dame."
Milton.

Counsel, see Consus.

Creditors, see Jani.

Crow, see Coronis.

Cultivated Land, see Sylvester.

Cup-bearer, see Ganymede.

Cupid (Cu′pid), the god of love, was the son of Jupiter and Venus. He is represented as a naked, winged boy, with a bow and arrows, and a torch. When he grew up to be a man he married Psyche.

"For Venus did but boast one only son,
And rosy Cupid was that boasted one;
He, uncontroll'd, thro' heaven extends his sway,
And gods and goddesses by turns obey."
Eusden, 1713.

Cuvera (Cuve′ra). The Indian god of wealth corresponding to the Greek Plutus.

Cybele (Cy′bele). The mother of the gods, and hence called Magna Mater. She was wife of Saturn. She is sometimes referred to under the names of Ceres, Rhea, Ops, and Vesta. She is represented as ri-

ding in a chariot drawn by lions. In one hand she holds a scepter, and in the other a key. On her head is a castelated crown, to denote that she was the first to protect castles and walls with towers.
"Nor Cybele with half so kind an eye
Surveyed her sons and daughters of the sky."
Dryden.

"Might she the wise Latona be,
Or the towered Cybele,
Mother of a hundred gods,
Juno dares not give her odds."
Milton.

Cyclops (Cy′clops) or Cyclopes (Cy′clopes) were the gigantic, one-eyed workmen of Vulcan, who made Jove's thunderbolts. Hesiod gives their names as Arges, Brontes, and Steropes.
"Meantime, the Cyclop raging with his wound,
Spreads his wide arms, and searches round and round."
Pope.

Cygnus (Cyg′nus), the bosom friend of Phaeton. He died of grief on the death of his friend, and was turned into a swan.
Cyllaros (Cyll′aros), one of Castor's horses. The color is mentioned as being coal-black, with white legs and tail. See Cillaros.
Cyllo (Cyl′lo). The name of one of Actaeon's hounds, which was lame.
Cyllopotes (Cyllop′otes). A name given to one of Actaeon's hounds which limped.

Cynosure (Cyn'osure). One of the nurses of Jupiter, turned by the god into a conspicuous constellation.
"Towers and battlements it sees
Bosomed high in tufted trees,
Where perhaps some beauty lies,
The Cynosure of neighboring eyes."
Milton.

Cyparissus (Cyparis'sus). A boy of whom Apollo was very fond; and when he died he was changed, at Apollo's intercession, into a cypress tree, the branches of which typify mourning.
Cypress (Cy'press), see Cyparissus.
Cypria (Cy'pria). A name of Venus, because she was worshiped in the island of Cyprus.
Cythera (Cyth'era). A name of Venus, from the island to which she was wafted in the shell.
Dactyli (Dacty'li) were priests of Cybele. They were given the name, because, like the fingers, they were ten in number.
Daedalus (Daed'alus) was a great architect and sculptor. He invented the wedge, the axe, the level, and the gimlet, and was the first to use sails. Daedalus also constructed the famous labyrinth for Minos, King of Crete. See Icarus.
"Now Daedalus, behold, by fate assigned,
A task proportioned to thy mighty mind."
Pope.

Dagon (Da'gon). A god of the Philistines, half man half fish, like the mermaid. Milton describes him as "Upward man and downward fish."
Dahak (Da'hak). The Persian devil.
Daityas (Dai'tyas). In Hindoo mythology the devils or evil gods.

Danae (Dan'ae) was a daughter of Acrisius and Eurydice. She had a son by Jupiter, who was drifted out to sea in a boat, but was saved by Polydectes and educated.

Fountain of Cybele (Rhea)
Danaides (Dana'ides), see Danaus.
Danaus (Dana'us), King of Argos, was the father of fifty daughters, who, all but one, at the command of their father, slew their husbands directly after marriage. For this crime they were condemned to the task of forever trying to draw water with vessels without any bottoms. See Hypermnestra.
Dancing, see Terpsichore.
Dangers, see Charybdis, also Scylla.
Daphne (Daph'ne). The goddess of the earth. Apollo courted her, but she fled from him, and was, at her own request, turned into a laurel tree.
"... As Daphne was
Root-bound, that fled Apollo."
Milton.

Dardanus (Dar'danus), a son of Jupiter, who built the city of Dardania, and by some writers was accounted the founder of Troy.

Dead-toll, see Charon.

Death, see Nox.

Deceiver, The, see Apaturia.

Deianira (Deiani'ra), daughter of Oeneus, was wife of Hercules. See Hercules.

Delius (De'lius), a name of Apollo, from the island in which he was born.

Delphi (Del'phi). A town on Mount Parnassus, famous for its oracle, and for a temple of Apollo. See Delphos.

Delphicus (Del'phicus). A name of Apollo, from Delphi.

Delphos (Del'phos), the place where the temple was built, from which the oracle of Apollo was given.

Demarus (De'marus). The Phoenician name of Jupiter.

Demogorgon (De'mogor'gon) was the tyrant genius of the soil or earth, the life and support of plants. He was depicted as an old man covered with moss, and was said to live underground. He is sometimes called the king of the elves and fays.

"Which wast begot in Demogorgon's hall
And saw'st the secrets of the world unmade."
Spenser.

Deucalion (Deuca'lion), one of the demi-gods, son of Prometheus and Pyrra. He and his wife, by making a ship, survived the deluge which Jupiter sent on the earth, circa 1503 B.C.

Devil, see Dahak, Daityas, and Obambou.

Diana (Di'ana), goddess of hunting and of chastity. She was the sister of Apollo, and daughter of Jupiter and Latona. She was known among the Greeks as Diana or Phoebe, and was honored as a triform goddess. As a celestial divinity she was called Luna; as a terrestrial Diana or Dictynna; and in the infernal regions Hecate.

Dictynna (Dictyn'na), a Greek name of Diana as a terrestrial goddess.

Dido (Di'do). A daughter of Belus, King of Tyre. It was this princess who bought a piece of land in Africa as large as could be encompassed by a bullock's hide, and when the purchase was completed, cut the hide into strips, and so secured a large tract of land. Here she built Carthage; and Virgil tells that when Aeneas was shipwrecked on the neighboring coast she received him with every kindness, and at last fell in love with him. But Aeneas did not reciprocate her affections, and this so grieved her that she stabbed herself. A tale is told in Facetiae Cantabrigienses of Professor Porson, who being one of a set party, the conversation turned on the subject of punning, when Porson observing that he could pun on any subject, a person present defied him to do so on the Latin gerunds, di, do, dum, which, however, he immediately did in the following admirable couplet:
"When Dido found Aeneas would not come,
She mourned in silence, and was Dido dumb."

Dies Pater (Di'es Pa'ter), or Father of the Day, a name of Jupiter.
Dii Selecti (Dii Selec'ti) composed the second class of gods. They were Coelus, Saturn, Genius, Oreus, Sol, Bacchus, Terra, and Luna.
Dindymene (Din'dyme'ne). A name of Cybele, from a mountain where she was worshiped.
"Nor Dindymene, nor her priest possest,
Can with their sounding cymbals shake the breast
Like furious anger."
Francis.

Diomedes (Diome'des), the cruel tyrant of Thrace, who fed his mares on the flesh of his guests. He was overcome by Hercules, and himself given to the same horses as food.
Dione (Dio'ne). A poetic name of Venus.

Dionysia (Diony'sia) were festivals in honor of Bacchus.
Dionysius (Diony'sius). A name of Bacchus, either from his father Jupiter (Dios), or from his nurses, the nymphs called Nysae.
Dioscuri (Dios'curi). Castor and Pollux, the sons of Jupiter.
Dirae (Di'rae). A name of the Furies.
Dis. A name of Pluto, god of hell, signifying riches.

"... That fair field
Of Enna, where Proserpine gathering flowers,
Herself a fairer flower, by gloomy Dis
Was gathered."
Milton.

Discord, see Ate.
Discordia (Discor'dia), sister of Nemesis, the Furies, and Death, was driven from heaven for having sown discord among the gods.
Diseases, see Pandora.
Distaff, see Pallas.
Dithyrambus. A surname of Bacchus.
Dodona (Dodo'na) was a celebrated oracle of Jupiter.

"O where, Dodona, is thine aged grove,
Prophetic fount, and oracle divine?"
Byron.

Dodonaeus (Dodonae'us). A name of Jupiter, from the city of Dodona.
Dog, see Lares.
Dolabra (Dola'bra). The knife used by the priests to cut up the sacrifices.
Dolphin, see Arion.
Doorga (Door'ga). A Hindoo goddess.
Doris (Do'ris) was daughter of Oceanus, and sister of Nereus, two of

the marine deities. From these two sisters sprang the several tribes of water nymphs.

Doto (Do'to). One of the Nereids or sea nymphs.

Draco (Dra'co). One of Actaeon's hounds.

Dragon, seven-headed, see Geryon.

Dreams, see Morpheus.

Dryads (Dry'ads) were rural deities, the nymphs of the forests, to whom their votaries offered oil, milk, and honey.

"Flushed with resistless charms he fired to love
Each nymph and little Dryad of the grove."
Ticknell.

Dumbness (Dumb'ness), see Atys.

Dweurgar (Dweur'gar). Scandinavian god of the Echo—a pigmy.

Eacus (E'acus), son of Jupiter and Egina, one of the judges of the infernal regions, who was appointed to judge the Europeans. See Aeacus.

Earth, see Antaeus.

Eblis (Eb'lis), the Mohammedan evil genius.

Echidna (Echid'na). A woman having a serpent's tail. She was the reputed mother of Chimaera, and also of the many-headed dog Orthos, of the three-hundred-headed dragon of the Hesperides, of the Colchian dragon, of the Sphinx, of Cerberus, of Scylla, of the Gorgons, of the Lernaean Hydra, of the vulture that gnawed away the liver of Prometheus, and also of the Nemean lion; in fact, the mother of all adversity and tribulation.

Echnobas (Echno'bas), one of Actaeon's hounds.

Echo (Ech'o) was a nymph who fell in love with Narcissus. But when he languished and died she pined away from grief and died also, preserving nothing but her voice, which repeats every sound that reaches her. Another fable makes Echo a daughter of Air and Tellus. She was partly deprived of speech by Juno, being allowed only to reply to questions.

"Sweet Echo, sweetest nymph, that liv'st unseen
Within thy airy shell.

. . . .

Sweet queen of parley, daughter of the sphere,
So may'st thou be translated to the skies,
And give resounding grace to all heaven's harmonies."
Milton.

"Oft by Echo's tedious tales misled."
Ovid.

Egeon. A giant sea-god, who assisted the Titans against Jupiter.
Egeria (Ege'ria). A nymph who is said to have suggested to Numa all his wise laws. She became his wife, and at his death was so disconsolate, and shed so many tears, that Diana changed her into a fountain.
Egil (E'gil). The Vulcan of northern mythology.
Egipans (Egip'ans) were rural deities who inhabited the forests and mountains, the upper half of the body being like that of a man, and the lower half like a goat.
Egis (E'gis) was the shield of Minerva. It obtained its name because it was covered with the skin of the goat Amalthaea, which nourished Jupiter. See Aegis.
Eleusinian Mysteries (Eleusin'ian). Religious rites in honor of Ceres, performed at Eleusis, in Attica.
Elysium (Elys'ium), or the Elysian Fields. The temporary abode of the just in the infernal regions.
Empyrean, The (Empyre'an). The fifth heaven, the seat of the heathen deity.
Endymion (Endym'ion). A shepherd, who acquired from Jupiter the faculty of being always young. One of the lovers of Diana.

Entertainments, see Comus.

Envy, see Furies.

Enyo was the Grecian name of Bellona, the goddess of war and cruelty.

Eolus (E'olus), see Aeolus.

Eos (E'os). The Grecian name of Aurora.

Eous (E'ous). One of the four horses which drew the chariot of Sol, the sun. The word is Greek, and means red.

Ephialtes (Eph'ial'tes). A giant who lost his right eye in an encounter with Hercules, and the left eye was destroyed by Apollo.

Erato (Er'ato). One of the Muses, the patroness of light poetry; she presided over the triumphs and complaints of lovers, and is generally represented as crowned with roses and myrtle, and holding a lyre in her hand.

Erebus (Er'ebus), son of Chaos, one of the gods of Hades, sometimes alluded to as representing the infernal regions.

Ergatis (Erga'tis). A name given to Minerva. It means the work-woman, and was given to the goddess because she was credited with having invented spinning and weaving.

Erictheus (Eric'theus), fourth King of Athens, was the son of Vulcan.

Erinnys (Erin'nys). A Greek name of the Furies. It means Disturber of the Mind.

Erisichthon (Erisich'thon) was punished with perpetual hunger because he defiled the groves of Ceres, and cut down one of the sacred oaks.

Eros (Er'os). The Greek god of love.

Erostratus (Eros'tratus). The rascal who burnt the temple of Diana at Ephesus, thereby hoping to make his name immortal.

Erycina (Eryc'ina). A name of Venus, from Mount Eryx in Sicily.

Erythreos (Erythre'os). The Grecian name of one of the horses of Sol's chariot.

Esculapius (Escula'pius), see Aesculapius.

Eta (E'ta), see Aeetes.

Ethon (E'thon), one of the horses who drew the chariot of Sol—the sun. The word is Greek, and signifies hot.

Etna (Et'na). A volcanic mountain, beneath which, according to Virgil, there is buried the giant Typhon, who breathes forth devouring flames.

Eudromos (Eu'dromos). The name of one of Actaeon's hounds.

Eulalon (Eu'lalon), one of the names of Apollo.

Eumenides (Eume'nides), a name of the Furies, meaning mild, and referring to the time when they were approved by Minerva.

Euphrosyne (Euphro'syne), one of the three Graces, see Graces.

"Come, thou goddess fair and free,
In heaven ycleped Euphrosyne."
Milton.

Eurus (Eu'rus). The east wind. A son of Aeolus.

Euryale (Eury'ale) was one of the Gorgons, daughter of Phorcus and Ceto.

Eurydice (Euryd'ice), wife of Orpheus, who was killed by a serpent on her wedding night.

"Nor yet the golden verge of day begun.
When Orpheus (her unhappy lord),
Eurydice to life restored,
At once beheld, and lost, and was undone."
F. Lewis.

Eurythion (Euryth'ion). A seven-headed dragon. See Geryon.

Euterpe (Eu'terpe), one of the Muses, the patroness of instrumental music. The word means agreeable.

Euvyhe (Eu'vyhe), an expression meaning "Well done, son." Jupiter so frequently addressed his son Bacchus by those words that the phrase at last became one of his names.

Evening Star, see Hesperus.

Evil, see Cacodaemon.

Evils, see Pandora.

Eye, of one, see Cyclops and Glaukopis.

Fame was a poetical deity, represented as having wings and blowing a trumpet. A temple was dedicated to her by the Romans.

Fate, see Nereus.

Fates, or Parcae, were the three daughters of Necessity. Their names were Clotho, who held the distaff; Lachesis, who turned the spindle; and Atropos, who cut the thread with the fatal shears.

Faun. A rural divinity, half man and half goat. They were very similar to the Satyrs. The Fauns attended the god Pan, and the Satyrs attended Bacchus.

Favonius (Favo'nius). The wind favorable to vegetation, that is, Zephyr—the west wind.

"... Time will run
On smoother, till Favonius reinspire
The frozen earth, and clothe in fresh attire
The lily and the rose, that neither sowed nor spun."
Milton.

Fays.
"The yellow-skirted Fays
Fly after the night-steeds,
Leaving their moon-loved maze."
Milton.

Feasts, see Comus.

Febris (Fe'bris) (fever), one of the evil deities, was worshiped that she might not do harm.

Februus (Feb'ruus). A name of Pluto, from the part of the funeral rites which consisted of purifications.

Feronia (Fero'nia), the Roman goddess of orchards, was patroness of enfranchised slaves. Some authors think Feronia is the same as Juno.

Fertility, see Lupercus.

Festivals, see Thalia.

Fidelity, see Iolaus.

Fides (Fi'des), the goddess of faith and honesty, and a temple in the Capitol of Rome.

Fine Arts, see Minerva.

Fire, see Salamander, Vesta, and Vulcan.

Fire Insurance, see Canopus.

Fisherman, see Glaucus.

Flath-innis (Flath'-in'nis), in Celtic mythology, is Paradise.

Fleece, Golden, see Golden Fleece, Argonauts, and Jason.

Flies, see Muscarius.

Flocks, see Pales (goddess of pastures).

Flora (Flo'ra), goddess of flowers and gardens, was wife of Zephyrus. She enjoyed perpetual youth. Her Grecian name was Chloris.

Floralia (Flora'lia) were licentious games instituted in honor of the goddess Flora.

Flowers, see Flora, Chloris, Hortensis, and Zephyrus.

Flute, see Marsyas.

Fortuna (Fortu'na), the goddess of fortune, had a temple erected to her by Servius Tullius. She was supposed to be able to bestow riches or poverty on mankind, and was esteemed one of the most potent of the ancient goddesses. She is usually represented as standing on a wheel, with a bandage over her eyes, and holding a cornucopia.

Fraud, one of the evil deities, was represented as a goddess with a human face and a serpent's body, and at the end of her tail was a scorpion's sting. She lived in the river Cocytus, and nothing but her head was ever seen.

Freyr (Frey'r). The Scandinavian god of fertility and peace. The patron god of Sweden and Iceland.

Freyja (Frey′ja). The Scandinavian Venus. The goddess of love.

Friga (Fri′ga). The Saxon goddess of earthly enjoyments. The name Friday is derived from her. In Scandinavian mythology she is the goddess of marriage.

Fro. The Scandinavian god of tempests and winds.

Frogs, see Clowns of Lycia.

The Fates

Fruits, see Ceres, and Pomona.

Funerals, see Libitina, and Manes.

Furies, The, were the three daughters of Acheron and Nox. They were the punishers of evil-doers. Their names were Tisiphone, Megaera, and Alecto, and were supposed to personify rage, slaughter, and envy.

Futurity, see Cassandra.

Gabriel (Ga'briel), in Jewish mythology is the prince of fire and thunder, and the angel of death to the favored people of God.

Galataea (Galatae'a). A sea nymph. Polyphemus, one of the Cyclops, loved her, but she disdained his attentions and became the lover of Acis, a Sicilian shepherd.

Gallantes (Gallan'tes), madmen, from Galli (which see).

Galli (Gal'li) were priests of Cybele who used to cut their arms with knives when they sacrificed, and acted so like madmen that demented people got the name of Gallantes.

Ganesa (Gan'esa). The Indian Mercury. The god of wisdom and prudence.

Ganga. One of the three Indian river goddesses.

Ganymede, a beautiful Phrygian youth, son of Tros, King of Troy. He succeeded Hebe in the office of cup-bearer to Jupiter. He is generally represented sitting on the back of a flying eagle.

Gardens, see Pomona (goddess of fruit-trees).

Gates, see Janus.

Gautama (Gau'tama) (Buddha). The chief deity of Burmah.

Genii were domestic divinities. Every man was supposed to have two of these genii accompanying him; one brought him happiness, the other misery.

Genitor (Gen'itor). A Lycian name of Jupiter.

Geometry, see Mercury.

Geryon (Ge'ryon) was a triple-bodied monster who lived at Gades, where his numerous flocks were guarded by Orthos, a two-headed dog, and by Eurythion, a seven-headed dragon. These guardians were destroyed by Hercules, and the cattle taken away.

Gimlet, see Daedalus.

Girdle, see Cestus (Venus's).

Glaucus (Glau'cus) was a fisherman who became a sea-god through eating a sea-weed, which he thought invigorated the fishes and might strengthen him.

Glaukopis (Glauko'pis). A name given to Minerva, because she had blue eyes.

Gnomes (Gno'mes), a name given by Plato to the invisible deities who were supposed to inhabit the earth.

Gnossis (Gnos′sis), a name given to Ariadne, from the city of Gnossus, in Crete.

Goat, see Iphigenia, Mendes, and Venus.

Goat's Feet, see Capripedes.

Golden Apple, see Atalanta.

Golden Fleece, The, was a ram's hide, sometimes described as white, and at other times as purple and golden. It was given to Phryxus, who carried it to Colchis, where King Aeetes entertained Phryxus, and the hide was hung up in the grove of Mars. Jason and forty-nine companions fetched back the golden fleece. See Argonauts.

Gopya (Gopy′a). Indian mythological nymphs.

Gorgons, The (Gor′gons), were three sisters, named Stheno, Euryale, and Medusa. They petrified every one they looked at. Instead of hair their heads were covered with vipers. Perseus conquered them, and cut off the head of Medusa, which was placed on the shield of Minerva, and all who fixed their eyes thereon were turned into stone.

Graces, The, were the attendants of Venus. Their names were, Aglaia, so called from her beauty and goodness; Thalia, from her perpetual freshness; and Euphrosyne, from her cheerfulness. They are generally depicted as three cheerful maidens with hands joined, and either nude or only wearing transparent robes—the idea being that kindnesses, as personified by the Graces, should be done with sincerity and candor, and without disguise. They were supposed to teach the duties of gratitude and friendship, and they promoted love and harmony among mankind.

Graces (fourth), see Pasithea.

Gradivus (Grad′ivus). A name given to Mars by the Romans. It meant the warrior who defended the city against all external enemies.

Gragus (Gra′gus). The name by which Jupiter was worshiped in Lycia.

Granaries, see Tutelina.

Grapsios (Grap′sios). A Lycian name of Jupiter.

Grasshopper, see Tithonus.

Grief, see Niobe.

Hada (Ha′da). The Babylonian Juno.

Hades (Ha′des). The Greek name of Pluto, the god of hell, the word signifying hidden, dark, and gloomy; the underworld, or infernal regions; sometimes written Ades.

Hailstorms, see Nuriel.

Halcyone (Halcy′one) (or Alcyone), one of the Pleiades, was a daughter of Aeolus.

Halcyons (Halcy′ons) were sea birds, supposed to be the Greek king-fishers. They made their nests on the waves, and during the period of incubation the sea was always calm. Hence the modern term Halcyon Days.

Hamadryades (Hamadry′ades) were wood-nymphs, who presided over trees.

Happiness, see Genii.

Haroeris (Haroe′ris). The Egyptian god, whose eyes are the sun and moon.

Harpies, The (Har′pies), (literally, snatchers, demons of destruction, or, in the modern sense, extortioners). They were monsters, half-birds, half-maidens, having the heads and breasts of women, the bodies of birds, and the claws of lions. Their names were Aello, Ocypete, and Celeno. They were loathsome creatures, living in filth, and poisoning everything they came in contact with.

"Such fiends to scourge mankind, so fierce, so fell,
Heaven never summoned from the depth of hell.
A virgin face, with wings and hookèd claws,
Death in their eyes, and famine in their jaws,
While proof to steel their hides and plumes remain
We strike the impenetrable fiends in vain."

Harpikruti (Harpi′kruti). The Egyptian name of the god Harpocrates.

Harpocrates (Harpoc′rates), or Horus, an Egyptian god, son of Osiris and Isis. He was the god of silence and secrecy. He is usually represented as a young man, holding a finger of one hand to his lips (expressive of a command to preserve silence), while in the other hand he holds a cornucopia, signifying early vegetation.

Harvest, see Segetia. A Roman divinity, invoked by the husbandman that the harvest might be plentiful.

Hawk, see Nysus.

Hazis (Ha´zis). The Syrian war-god.

Health, see Hygeia and Salus.

Heaven, Queen of, (Hea´ven) see Belisama. God of, see Coelus.

Hebe (He´be), daughter of Zeus (Jupiter) and Hera (Juno), was the goddess of youth. She was cup-bearer to Jupiter and the gods, until she had an awkward fall at a festival, causing her to alight in an indecent posture, which so displeased Jupiter that she was deprived of her office, and Ganymede was appointed in her stead.

"Wreathed smiles,
Such as hung on Hebe's cheek,
And love to live in dimples sleek."
Milton.

"Bright Hebe waits; by Hebe ever young
The whirling wheels are to the chariot hung."
Pope.

Hecate (Hec´ate). There were two goddesses known by this name, but the one generally referred to in modern literature is Hecate, or Proserpine, the name by which Diana was known in the infernal regions. In heaven her name was Luna, and her terrestrial name was Diana. She was a moon-goddess, and is generally represented in art with three bodies, standing back to back, a torch, a sword, and a lance in each right hand.

Hecuba (Hec′uba). The wife of Priam, king of Troy, and mother of Paris. Taken captive in the Trojan war, she fell to the lot of Ulysses after the destruction of Troy, and was afterwards changed into a hound.

"What's Hecuba to him, or he to Hecuba?"
Shakespeare.

Heifer, see Ino.

Helena (Hel′ena) when a child was so beautiful that Theseus and Perithous stole her, but she was restored by Castor and Pollux. She became the wife of Menelaus, king of Sparta, but eloped with Paris, and thus caused the Trojan War. After the death of Paris she married Deiphobus, his brother, and then betrayed him to Menelaus. She was afterward tied to a tree and strangled by order of Polyxo, king of Rhodes.

Heliades, The (He′liades), were the daughters of Sol, and the sisters of Phaeton, at whose death they were so sad that they stood mourning till they became metamorphosed into poplar trees, and their tears were turned into amber.

Helicon (Hel′icon). A mountain in Boeotia sacred to the Muses, from which place the fountain Hippocrene flowed.

"Yet still the doting rhymer dreams,
And sings of Helicon's bright streams;
But Helicon for all his clatter
Yields only uninspiring water."
Broom, 1720.

Heliconiades (Helico′niades). A name given to the Muses, from Mount Helicon.

Heliopolis (Heliop′olis), in Egypt, was the city of the sun.

Helios (He′lios). The Grecian sun-god, or charioteer of the sun, who went home every evening in a golden boat which had wings.

Heliotrope (Hel′iotrope). Clytie was turned into this flower by Apollo. See Clytie.

Helle (Hel′le) was drowned in the sea, into which she fell from off the back of the golden ram, on which she and Phryxus were escaping from the oppression of their stepmother Ino. The episode gave the name of the Hellespont to the part of the sea where Helle was drowned, and it is now called the Dardanelles. She was the daughter of Athamas and Nephele.

Hellespontiacus (Hellespontia′cus). A title of Priapus.

Hemphta (Hemph′ta). The Egyptian god Jupiter.

Hephaestus (Hephaes′tus). The Greek Vulcan, the smith of the gods.

Hera (He′ra). The Greek name of Juno.

Heracles (Her′acles) is the same as Hercules.

Hercules (Her′cules) was the son of Jupiter and Alcmena. The goddess Juno hated him from his birth, and sent two serpents to kill him, but though only eight months old he strangled them. As he got older he was set by his master Eurystheus what were thought to be twelve impossible tasks which have long been known as the "Twelve Labors of Hercules." They were:

First, To slay the Nemean Lion.

Second, To destroy the Hydra which infested the marshes of Lerna.

Third, To bring to Eurystheus the Arcadian Stag with the golden horns and brazen hoofs.

Fourth, To bring to his master the Boar of Erymanthus.

Fifth, To cleanse the stable of King Augeas, in which 3,000 oxen had been kept for thirty years, but had never been cleaned out.

Sixth, To destroy the Stymphalides, terrible carnivorous birds.

Seventh, To capture the Bull which was desolating Crete.

Eighth, To capture the mares of Diomedes, which breathed fire from their nostrils, and ate human flesh.

Ninth, To procure the girdle of Hippolyte, queen of the Amazons.

Tenth, To bring to Eurystheus the flesh-eating oxen of Geryon, the monster king of Gades.

Eleventh, To bring away some of the golden apples from the garden of the Hesperides.

Twelfth, To bring up from Hades the three-headed dog, Cerberus.

All these tasks he successfully accomplished, and, besides, he assisted the gods in their wars with the giants. Several other wonderful feats are mentioned under other headings, as Antaeus, Cacus, etc. His death was brought about through his endeavors to preserve Deianira from the attacks of Nessus, the centaur, whom he killed. The centaur, before he expired, gave his mystic tunic to Deianira, who in turn gave it to Hercules, and he put it on, but his doing so brought on an illness of which he could not be cured. In a fit of desperation he cast himself into a funeral pile on Mount Oeta; but Jupiter had him taken to heaven in a four-horse chariot, and only the mortal part of Hercules was consumed.

"Let Hercules himself do what he may,
The cat will mew, and dog will have his day."
Shakespeare.

Herdsmen, see Bubona.

Hermae (Her'mae) were statues of Hermes (Mercury), which were set up in Athens for boundaries, and as direction marks for travelers.

Hermanubis (Her'manu'bis), see Anubis.

Hermathenae (Hermathe'nae) were statues of Mercury and Minerva placed together.

Hermes (Her'mes). A Greek name of the god Mercury.

"Hermes obeys. With golden pinions binds
His flying feet and mounts the western winds."
Virgil.

Hermione (Hermi'one), daughter of Mars and Venus, who was turned into a serpent, and allowed to live in the Elysian Fields. There was another Hermione, daughter of Menelaus and Helen; she was betrothed to Orestes, but was carried away by Pyrrhus, the son of Achilles.

Hero (He'ro). A priestess of Venus, with whom Leander was so enamored that he swam across the Hellespont every night to visit her, but at last was drowned; when Hero saw the fate of her lover she threw herself into the sea and was also drowned.

Heroes, see Valhalla.

Hesperides (Hesper'ides). Three daughters of Hesperus, King of Italy. They were appointed to guard the golden apples which Juno gave Jupiter on their wedding day. See Hercules.

Hesperus (Hes'perus), brother of Atlas, was changed into the evening star.

"To the ocean now I fly,
And those happy climes that lie
Where day never shuts his eye,
Upon the broad fields of the sky:
There I suck the liquid air,
All amidst the gardens fair
Of Hesperus and his daughters three,
That sing about the golden tree."
Milton.

Hestia (Hes'tia). The Greek name of Vesta, the goddess of the hearth.

Hieroglyphics (Hierogly'phics), see Mercury.

Highways, see Janus.

Hildur (Hil'dur). The Scandinavian Mars.

Hippia (Hip'pia). A surname of Minerva.

Hippius (Hip'pius). A surname of Neptune.

Hippocampus (Hippocam'pus). The name of Neptune's favorite horse, a fabulous marine animal, half horse and half fish.

Hippocrenides (Hippocre'nides), a name of the Muses, from the fountain of Hippocrene (the horse fountain), which was formed by a kick of the winged horse Pegasus.

Hippolyte (Hippol'yte), queen of the Amazons, daughter of Mars. Her father gave her a famous girdle, which Hercules was required to procure (see Hercules). She was conquered by Hercules, and given by him in marriage to Theseus.

Hippolytus (Hippol'ytus) was the son of Theseus and Hippolyte; he was killed by a fall from a chariot, but was raised to life again by Diana, or, as some say, by Aesculapius.

Hippona (Hippo'na) was a rural divinity, the goddess of horses.

History, see Clio and Saga.

Honey, see Aristaeus and Dryads.

Hope, see Pandora.

Horae (Ho'rae) were the daughters of Sol and Chronis, the goddesses of the seasons.

Horse, see Cyllaros.

Horse Races, see Neptune.

Horses, see Hippona.

Hortensis (Horten'sis), a name of Venus, because she looked after plants and flowers in gardens.

Horus (Ho'rus). The name of two deities, one Sol, the Egyptian day god; the other, the son of Osiris and Isis. See Harpocrates.

Hostilina (Hostil'ina). A rural divinity; goddess of growing corn.

Hunger, see Erisichthon.

Hunting, see Diana.

Huntsmen, see Pan.

Hebe

Hyacinthus (Hyacin′thus) was a boy greatly loved by Apollo; but he was accidentally slain by him with a quoit. Apollo caused to spring from his blood the flower Hyacinth.

Hyades (Hy′ades) were seven daughters of Atlas and Aethra, and they formed a constellation which, when it rises with the sun, threatens rain.

Hydra (Hy′dra). A monster serpent, which had a hundred heads. It was slain by Hercules. See Hercules.

Hygeia (Hyge′ia), the goddess of health, was a daughter of Aesculapius and Epione. She was represented as a young woman giving a serpent drink out of a saucer, the serpent being twined round her arm.

Hylas (Hy′las). A beautiful boy beloved by Hercules. The nymphs were jealous of him, and spirited him away while he was drawing water for Hercules. See Wm. Morris's tragedy, "The Life and Death of Jason."

Hymen (Hy'men), the Grecian god of marriage, was either the son of Bacchus and Venus, or, as some say, of Apollo and one of the Muses. He was represented as a handsome youth, holding in his hand a burning torch.

"Some few there are of sordid mould
Who barter youth and bloom for gold:
But Hymen, gen'rous, just, and kind,
Abhors the mercenary mind;
Such rebels groan beneath his rod,
For Hymen's a vindictive god."
Dr. Cotton, 1736.

Hymn, see Paean.
Hyperion (Hype'rion). Son of Coelus and Terra. The model of manly beauty, synonymous with Apollo. The personification of the sun.
"So excellent a king; that was to this
Hyperion to a satyr."
Shakespeare.

Hypermnestra (Hypermnes'tra). One of the fifty daughters of Danaus, who were collectively called the Danaides. She was the one who refused to kill her husband on the wedding night. See Danaus.
Iacchus (Iac'chus). Another name for Bacchus.
Iapetos (Iap'etos). The father of Atlas. See Japetus.
Iblees (Ib'lees). The Arabian Satan.
Icarus (Ic'arus), son of Daedalus, who with his father made themselves wings with which to fly from Crete to escape the resentment of Minos. The wings were fixed to the shoulders by wax. Icarus flew too near the sun, and the heat melting the wax, caused the wings to drop off, and he fell into the Aegean or Icarian sea and was drow-

ned.

Ichnobate (Ichnoba'te). One of Actaeon's hounds; the word means tracker.

Idaea (Idae'a). A name of Cybele, from Mount Ida, where she was worshiped.

Idaean Mother (Idae'an Mother). Cybele was sometimes so called, in Cyprus, in which there is a grove sacred to Venus.

Idalia (Ida'lia). A name of Venus, from Mount Idalus, in Cyprus, in which there is a grove sacred to Venus.

Imperator (Impera'tor) was a name of Jupiter, given to him at Praeneste.

Inachus (I'nachus) was one of the earliest of the demi-gods or heroes, King of Argos.

Incendiary, see Erostratus.

Incense, see Venus.

Incubus (In'cubus). A Roman name of Pan, meaning The Nightmare. See Innus.

Indigetes (Indig'etes) were deified mortals, gods of the fourth order. They were peculiar to some district.

Indra (In'dra). The Hindoo Jupiter; his wife was Indrant, who presides over the winds and thunder.

Infants, see Natio.

Innus (In'nus). A name of Pan, the same as Incubus.

Ino (In'o), second wife of Athamas, King of Thebes, father of Phryxus and Helle. Ino had two children, who could not ascend the throne while Phryxus and Helle were alive. Ino therefore persecuted them to such a degree that they determined to escape. They did so on a ram, whose hide became the Golden Fleece (see Phryxus and Helle). Ino destroyed herself, and was changed by Neptune into a sea-goddess.

Inoa (Ino'a) were festivals in memory of Ino.

Instrumental Music, see Euterpe.

Io (I'o) was a daughter of Inachus, and a priestess of Juno at Argos. Jupiter courted her, and was detected by Juno, when the god turned

Io into a beautiful heifer. Juno demanded the beast of Jupiter, and set the hundred-eyed Argus to watch her. Jupiter persuaded Mercury to destroy Argus, and Io was set at liberty, and restored to human shape. Juno continued her persecutions, and Io had to wander from place to place till she came to Egypt, where she became wife of King Osiris, and won such good opinions from the Egyptians that after her death she was worshiped as the goddess Isis.

Iolaus (Iola'us), son of Iphicles, assisted Hercules in conquering the Hydra, by burning with hot irons the place where the heads were cut off; and for his assistance he was restored to youth by Hebe. Lovers used to go to his monument at Phocis and ratify their vows of fidelity.

Iothun (Io'thun). Celtic mythological monsters, or giants.

Iphicles (Iph'icles) was twin brother of Hercules, and father of Iolaus.

Iphigenia (Iphigeni'a) was a daughter of Agamemnon and Clytemnestra. Agamemnon made a vow to Diana, which involved the sacrifice of Iphigenia, but just at the critical moment she was carried to heaven, and a beautiful goat was found on the altar in her place.

Iris (I'ris), daughter of Thaumas and Electra, was the attendant of Juno, and one of the messengers of the gods. Her duty was to cut the thread which detained expiring souls. She is the personification of the rainbow.

Iron, see Vulcan.

Isis (I'sis), wife of Osiris, and a much worshiped divinity of the Egyptians. See Io.

Itys (I'tys) was killed by his mother Procne when six years old, and given to his father Tereus, a Thracian of Daulis, as food. The gods were so enraged at this that they turned Itys into a pheasant, Procne into a swallow, and Tereus into a hawk.

Ixion (Ixi'on), the son of Phlegyas, King of the Lapithae. For attempting to produce thunder, Jupiter cast him into hell, and had him bound to a wheel, surrounded with serpents, which is forever turning over a river of fire.

"The powers of vengeance, while they hear,

Touched with compassion, drop a tear;
Ixion's rapid wheel is bound,
Fixed in attention to the sound."
F. Lewis.

"Or, as Ixion fix'd, the wretch shall feel
The giddy motion of the whirling wheel."
Pope.

Jani (Ja′ni) was a place in Rome where there were three statues of Janus, and it was a meeting-place for usurers and creditors.

Janitor (Ja′nitor). A title of Janus, from the gates before the doors of private houses being called Januae.

Janus (Ja′nus). A king of Italy, said to have been the son of Coelus, others say of Apollo; he sheltered Saturn when he was driven from heaven by Jupiter. Janus presided over highways, gates, and locks, and is usually represented with two faces, because he was acquainted with the past and the future; or, according to others, because he was taken for the sun, who opens the day at his rising, and shuts it at his setting. A brazen temple was erected to him in Rome, which was always open in time of war, and closed during peace.

"Old Janus, if you please,
Grave two-faced father."

"In two-faced Janus we this moral find,—
While we look forward, we should glance behind."
Colman.

Japetus (Jap'etus), son of Coelus and Terra, husband of Clymene. He was looked upon by the Greeks as the father of all mankind. See Iapetos.

Jason (Ja'son), the son of Aeson, king of Iolcos; he was brought up by the centaur Chiron. His uncle Aeeta sent him to fetch the Golden Fleece from Colchis (see Argonauts). He went in the ship Argo with forty-nine companions, the flower of Greek youth. With the help of Juno they got safe to Colchis, but the King Aeetes promised to restore the Golden Fleece only on condition that the Argonauts performed certain services. Jason was to tame the wild fiery bulls, and to make them plow the field of Mars; to sow in the ground the teeth of a serpent, from which would spring armed men who would fight against him who plowed the field of Mars; to kill the fiery dragon which guarded the tree on which the Golden Fleece was hung. The fate of Jason and the rest of the Argonauts seemed certain; but Medea, the king's daughter, fell in love with Jason, and with the help of charms which she gave him he overcame all the difficulties which the king had put in his way. He took away the Golden Fleece and Medea also. The king sent his son Absyrtus to overtake the fugitives, but Medea killed him, and strewed his limbs in his father's path, so that he might be delayed in collecting them, and this enabled Jason and Medea to escape. After a time Jason got tired of Medea, and married Glauce, which cruelty Medea revenged by killing her children before their father's eyes. Jason was accidentally killed by a beam of the ship Argo falling on him.

Jocasta (Jocas'ta) (otherwise Epicasta), wife of Laius, King of Thebes, who in after-life married her own son, Oedipus, not knowing who he was, and, on discovering the fatal mistake, hanged herself.

Jove. A very general name of Jupiter.

"From the great father of the gods above
My muse begins, for all is full of Jove."
Virgil.

Judges in Hell, The, were Rhadamanthus for Asiatics; Aeacus for Europeans; Minos was the presiding judge in the infernal regions. See Triptolemus.

Jugatinus (Jugatin'us) was one of the nuptial deities.

Juno (Ju'no) was the daughter of Saturn and Ops, alias Cybele. She was married to Jupiter, and became queen of all the gods and goddesses, and mistress of heaven and earth. Juno was the mother of Mars, Vulcan, Hebe, and Lucina. She prompted the gods to conspire against Jupiter, but the attempt was frustrated, and Apollo and Neptune were banished from heaven by Jupiter. Juno is the goddess of marriage, and the protectress of married women; and she had special regard for virtuous women. In the competition for the celebrated Golden Apple, which Juno, Venus, and Minerva each claimed as the fairest among the goddesses, Juno was much displeased when Paris gave the apple to Venus. The goddess is generally represented riding in a chariot drawn by peacocks, with a diadem on her head, and a scepter in her hand.

Jupiter (Ju'piter), son of Saturn and Cybele (or Ops), was born on Mount Ida, in Crete, and nourished by the goat Amalthaea. When quite young Jupiter rescued his father from the Titans; and afterward, with the help of Hercules, defeated the giants, the sons of earth, when they made war against heaven. Jupiter was worshiped with great solemnity under various names by most of the heathen nations. The Africans called him Ammon; the Babylonians, Belus; and the Egyptians, Osiris (see Jove). He is represented as a majestic personage seated on a throne, holding in his hands a scepter and a thunderbolt; at his feet stood a spread eagle.

Justice, see Astrea, Nemesis.

Kali. A Hindoo goddess, after whom Calicut is named.

Kaloc (Ka'loc). One of the chief of the Mexican gods.

Kama (Kam'a). The Hindoo god of love.

Kebla (Keb'la). The point of the compass which worshipers look to during their invocations. Thus the Sol or Sun worshipers turn to the east, where the sun rises, and the Mohammedans turn toward Mecca.

Kederli (Ke'derli), in Mohammedan mythology, is a god corresponding to the English St. George, and is still invoked by the Turks when they go to war.

Kiun (Ki'un). The Egyptian Venus.

Kneph. An Egyptian god, having a ram's head and a man's body.

Krishna (Krish'na). An Indian god, the revenger of wrongs; also called the Indian Apollo.

Krodo (Kro'do). The Saxon Saturn.

Kumara (Ku'ma'ra). The war-god of the Hindoos.

Kuvera (Ku'vera). The Hindoo god of riches.

Labe (La'be). The Arabian Circe, who had unlimited power of metamorphosis.

Labor (Lab'or), see Atlas, Hercules.

Labyrinth, see Theseus.

Lachesis (Lach'esis). One of the three goddesses of Fate, the Parcae. She spun the thread of life.

Lacinia (Lacin'ia). A name of Juno.

Lactura. One of the goddesses of growing corn.

Ladon (La'don). The dragon which guarded the apples in the garden of the Hesperides. Also the name of one of Actaeon's hounds. Also the river in Arcadia to which Syrinx fled when pursued by Pan, where she was changed into a reed, and where Pan made his first pipe.

Laelaps (Lae'laps). One of Diana's hunting-dogs, which, while pursuing a wild boar, was petrified. Also the name of one of Actaeon's hounds.

Laksmi (Laks'mi) Hindoo goddess of wealth and pleasure. One of the husbands of Vishnu.

Lamentation, see Cocytus.

Lamia (Lam'ia). An evil deity among the Greeks and Romans, and the great dread of their children, whom she had the credit of constantly enticing away and destroying.

Lamp, see Lares and Penates.

Lampos (Lam′pos). One of Aurora's chariot horses, the other being Phaeton.

Laocoon (Laoc′oon). One of the priests of Apollo, who was, with his two sons, strangled to death by serpents, because he opposed the admission of the fatal wooden horse to Troy.

Laomedon (Laom′edon), son of Ilus, a Trojan king. He was famous for having, with the assistance of Apollo and Neptune, built the walls of Troy.

Lapis (Lap′is). The oath stone. The Romans used to swear by Jupiter Lapis.

Lapithus (Lap′ithus), son of Apollo. His numerous children were called Lapithae, and they are notorious for their fight with the centaurs at the nuptial feast of Perithous and Hippodamia.

Lares and Penates (La′res and Pena′tes) were sons of Mercury and Lara, or, as other mythologists say, of Jupiter and Lamida. They belonged to the lower order of Roman gods, and presided over homes and families. Their statues were generally fixed within the doors of houses, or near the hearths. Lamps were sacred to them, as symbols of vigilance, and the dog was their sacrifice.

Lark, see Scylla and Nysus.

Latona (Lato′na), daughter of Coelus and Phoebe, mother of Apollo and Diana. Being admired so much by Jupiter, Juno was jealous, and Latona was the object of the goddess' constant persecution.

Laughter, see Momus and Venus.

Laurel (Lau′rel), see Daphne.

Laverna (Laver′na). The Roman patroness of thieves.

Law, see Menu.

Lawgiver, see Nomius.

Laws, see Themis.

Leander (Lean′der), see Hero.

Leather Bottle, see Ascolia.

Leda (Le′da) was the mother of Castor and Pollux, their father being Jupiter, in the shape of a swan. After her death she received the name of Nemesis.

Lemnius (Lem′nius). One of the names of Vulcan.

Lemures (Lem′ures). The ghosts of departed souls. Milton, in his "Ode to the Nativity," says—

"Lemures moan with midnight plaint."

They are sometimes referred to as the Manes of the dead.

Lenaeus (Lenae′us). One of the names of Bacchus.

Lerna (Ler′na). The lake or swamp near Argos where Hercules conquered the Lernaean Hydra.

Lethe (Le′the). One of the rivers of the infernal regions, of which the souls of the departed are obliged to drink to produce oblivion or forgetfulness of everything they did or knew while alive on the earth.

"A slow and silent stream,
Lethe, the river of oblivion, rolls
Her watery labyrinth, whereof who drinks
Forthwith his former state and being forgets,
Forgets both joy and grief, pleasure and pain."
Milton.

Hera

Leucothea (Leucoth'ea). The name of Ino after she was transformed into a sea nymph.

Levana (Leva'na). The deity who presided over new-born infants.

Level, The, see Daedalus.

Liakura (Liak'ura). Mount Parnassus.

Liberal Arts, see Minerva.

Liber Pater (Li'ber Pa'ter). A name of Bacchus.

Liberty, see Bacchus.

Libissa (Lib'issa). Queen of fays and fairies.

Libitina (Libiti'na). A Roman goddess, the chief of the funeral deities.

Licentiousness, see Belphegor.

Ligea (Lige'a). A Greek syren or sea-nymph, one of the Nereides.

Lightning, see Agni.

Lilith (Li'lith). A Jewish myth representing a finely dressed woman who is a great enemy to new-born children. She was said to have been Adam's first wife, but, refusing to submit to him, was turned from Paradise and made a specter.

Lina (Li′na). The goddess of the art of weaving.

Lindor (Lin′dor). A lover in the shape of a shepherd, like Corydon; a love-sick swain.

Lion, see Atalanta, Chimaera.

Liver, see Tityus and Prometheus.

Locks, see Janus.

Lofen (Lo′fen). The Scandinavian god who guards friendship.

Lofua (Lof′ua). The Scandinavian goddess who reconciles lovers.

Loke. The Scandinavian Satan, the god of strife, the spirit of evil. Written also Lok, and Loki.

Lotis (Lo′tis). A daughter of Neptune, who fled from Priapus, and only escaped from him by being transformed into a lotus-plant.

Lotus-Plant (Lo′tus-Plant), see Lotis.

Love, see Cupid, Eros, Venus.

Lucian (Lu′cian). The impersonation of folly, changed into an ass.

Lucifer (Lu′cifer). The morning star.

Lucina (Luci′na). The goddess who presides at the birth of children. She was a daughter of Jupiter and Juno, or, according to others, of Latona.

"Lucina, hail! So named from thine own grove,
Or from the light thou giv'st us from above."
Ovid.

Lud. In ancient British mythology the king of the Britons. He is said to have given his name to London.

Luna (Lu′na). The name of Diana as a celestial divinity. See Diana and Hecate. Also, the Italian goddess of the moon.

Lupercus (Lu′percus), or Pan. The Roman god of fertility; his festival day was 15th February, and the festivals were called Lupercalia.

Lycaonian Food (Lycaon′ian). Execrable viands, such as were supplied to Jupiter by Lycaon. To test the divine knowledge of the god he served up human flesh, which Jove discovered, and punished Lycaon by turning him into a wolf.

Lycian Clowns were turned into frogs by Latona or Ceres.

Lymniades (Lymni'ades). Nymphs who resided in marshes.

Lynceus (Lyn'ceus). One of the Argonauts. The personification of sharpsightedness.

Lyre. This musical instrument is constantly associated with the doings of the ancient deities. Amphion built the walls of Thebes by the music of his lyre. Arion charmed the dolphins in a similar way. Hercules broke the head of Linus, his music-master, with the lyre he was learning to use; and Orpheus charmed the most savage beasts, and even the Harpies and gods of the infernal regions, with the enchanting music of the stringed lyre. See Mercury.

Maenades (Maen'ades). Priestesses of Bacchus.

Magicians, see Telchines.

Magna Dea (Mag'na De'a), a name of Ceres.

Magpies, see Pierides.

Mahasoor (Ma'ha'soor). The Hindoo god of evil.

Maia (Ma'ia). The mother of the Grecian Mercury.

Mammon (Mam'mon). The money god.

Manes (Ma'nes). The souls of the departed. The Roman god of funerals and tombs.

"All have their Manes, and their Manes bear.
The few who're cleansed to those abodes repair,
And breathe in ample fields the soft Elysian air."

Manuring Land, see Picumnus.

March 24, Bellona's Day. See Bellona.

Marina (Mari'na). A name of Venus, meaning sea-foam, from her having been formed from the froth of the sea. See Aphrodite.

Marriage, see Cama, Hymen, Juno, Jugatinus.

Mars, the god of war, was the son of Jupiter and Juno. Venus was his favorite goddess, and among their children were Cupid, Anteros, and Harmonia. In the Trojan War Mars took the part of the Trojans, but was defeated by Diomedes. The first month of the old Roman year (our March) was sacred to Mars.

Marshes, see Lymniades.

Marsyas (Mar′syas). The name of the piper who challenged Apollo to a musical contest, and, being defeated, was flayed to death by the god. He was the supposed inventor of the flute.

Marut (Ma′rut). The Hindoo god of tempestuous winds.

Matura (Matu′ra). One of the rural deities who protected the growing corn at time of ripening.

Maximus (Max′imus). One of the appellations of Jupiter, being the greatest of the gods.

Measures and Weights, see Mercury.

Medea (Mede′a). Wife of Jason, chief of the Argonauts. To punish her husband for infidelity, Medea killed two of her children in their father's presence. She was a great sorceress. See Jason.

"Now to Medaea's dragons fix my reins."
F. Lewis.

"Let not Medea draw her murdering knife,
And spill her children's blood upon the stage."
Lord Roscommon.

Medicine, see Apollo.

Meditation, see Harpocrates.

Medusa (Medu′sa). One of the Gorgons. Minerva changed her beautiful hair into serpents. She was conquered by Perseus, who cut off her head, and placed it on Minerva's shield. Every one who looked at the head was turned into stone.

Ulysses, in the Odyssey, relates that he wished to see more of the inhabitants of Hades, but was afraid, as he says—
"Lest Gorgon, rising from the infernal lakes,
With horrors armed, and curls of hissing snakes,
Should fix me, stiffened at the monstrous sight,
A stony image in eternal night."
Pope.

"Medusa with Gorgonian terror guards
The ford."
Milton.

"Remove that horrid monster, and take hence
Medusa's petrifying countenance."
Addison.

Megaera (Meg'aera). One of the three Furies—Greek goddesses of vengeance.
Megale (Meg'ale). A Greek name of Juno, meaning great.
Melicerta (Melicer'ta), see Palaemon.
Mellona (Mello'na). One of the rural divinities, the goddess of bees.
Melpomene (Melpom'ene). One of the nine Muses, the goddess of tragedy.
Memnon (Mem'non), son of Tithonus and of Eos, who after the death of Hector brought the Aethiopians to the assistance of Priam in the war against Troy.
Memory, see Mnemosyne.
Mendes (Men'des). An Egyptian god like Pan. He was worshiped in

the form of a goat.

Menelaus (Menela'us). A Spartan king, brother of Agamemnon. The elopement of his wife Helen with Paris was the cause of the siege of Troy. See Helena.

Menu (Me'nu), or Manu (Ma'nu). The Hindoo law-giver. See Satyavrata.

Merchants, see Mercury.

Mercury (Mer'cury), the son of Jupiter and Maia, was the messenger of the gods, and the conductor of the souls of the dead to Hades. He was the supposed inventor of weights and measures, and presided over orators and merchants. Mercury was accounted a most cunning thief, for he stole the bow and quiver of Apollo, the girdle of Venus, the trident of Neptune, the tools of Vulcan, and the sword of Mars, and he was therefore called the god of thieves. He is the supposed inventor of the lyre, which he exchanged with Apollo for the Caduceus. There was also an Egyptian Mercury under the name of Thoth, or Thaut, who is credited with having taught the Egyptians geometry and hieroglyphics. Hermes is the Greek name of Mercury. In art he is usually represented as having on a winged cap, and with wings on his heels.

"And there, without the power to fly,
Stands fix'd a tip-toe Mercury."
Lloyd, 1750.

"Then fiery expedition be my wing,
Jove's Mercury, and herald for a king."

"Be Mercury, set feathers to thy heels
And fly, like thought, from them to me again."
Shakespeare.

Meru (Me′ru). The abode of the Hindoo god Vishnu. It is at the top of a mountain 8,000 leagues high. The Olympus of the East Indians.

Midas (Mi′das). A king of Phrygia, who begged of Bacchus the special gift that everything that he touched might be turned into gold. The request was granted, and as soon as he touched his food it also was turned to gold, and for fear of being starved he was compelled to ask the god to withdraw the power he had bestowed upon him. He was told to bathe in the river Pactolus. He did so, and the sands which he stood on were golden forever after. It was this same king who, being appointed to be judge in a musical contest between Apollo and Pan, gave the satyr the palm; whereupon Apollo, to show his contempt, bestowed on him a pair of asses' ears. This gave rise to the term "Midas-eared" as a synonym for ill-judged, or indiscriminate.
"He dug a hole, and in it whispering said,
What monstrous ears sprout from King Midas' head."
Ovid.

Milo (Mi′lo), a celebrated Croton athlete, who is said to have felled an ox with his fist, and to have eaten the beast in one day. His statue is often seen with one hand in the rift of a tree trunk, out of which he is vainly trying to withdraw it. The fable is, that when he got to be an old man he attempted to split an oak tree, but having lost his youthful vigor, the tree closed on his hand and he was held a prisoner till the wolves came and devoured him.

Mimallones (Mimallo′nes). The "wild women" who accompanied Bacchus, so called because they mimicked his actions, putting horns on their heads when they took part in his orgies.

Mimir (Mi′mir). In Scandinavian mythology the god of wisdom.

Mind, see Erinnys.

Minerva (Miner′va), the goddess of wisdom, war, and the liberal arts, is said to have sprung from the head of Jupiter fully armed for battle. She was a great benefactress of mankind, and patroness of the fine arts. She was the tutelar deity of the city of Athens. She is also known by the names of Pallas, Parthenos, Tritonia, and Glaukopis. She was very generally worshiped by the ancients, and her temple at Athens, the Parthenon, still remains. She is represented in statues and pictures as wearing a golden helmet encircled with an olive branch, and a breastplate. In her right hand she carries a lance, and by her side is the famous aegis or shield, covered with the skin of Amalthaea, the goat which nourished Jupiter; and for the boss of the shield is the head of Medusa. An owl, the emblem of meditation, is on the left; and a cock, the emblem of courage, on the right. The Elgin Marbles in the British Museum, London, were brought from the Parthenon, her temple at Athens.

Minos (Mi′nos). The supreme of the three judges of hell, before whom the spirits of the departed appeared and heard their doom.

Minotaur (Min′otaur). The monster, half man, half bull, which Theseus slew.

Mirth, see Momus.

Misery, see Genii.

Mithras (Mith′ras). A Persian divinity, the ruler of the universe, corresponding with the Roman Sol.

Mnemosyne (Mnemos′yne). Mother of the Muses and goddess of memory. Jupiter courted the goddess in the guise of a shepherd.

Moakibat (Moak′ibat). The recording angel of the Mohammedans.

Moloch (Mo′loch). A god of the Phoenicians to whom human victims, principally children, were sacrificed. Moloch is figurative of the influence which impels us to sacrifice that which we ought to cherish most dearly.

"First Moloch, horrid king, besmeared with blood
Of human sacrifice, and parents' tears,
Though for the noise of drums and timbrels loud,
Their children's cries unheard, that poured through fire
To this grim idol."
Milton.

Momus (Mo'mus). The god of mockery and blame. The god who blamed Jove for not having made a window in man's breast, so that his thoughts could be seen. His bitter jests occasioned his being driven from heaven in disgrace. He is represented as holding an image of Folly in one hand, and raising a mask from his face with the other. He is also described as the god of mirth or laughter.

Moneta (Mone'ta). A name given to Juno by those writers who considered her the goddess of money.

Money, see Moneta.

Money-God, see Mammon.

Moon. The moon was, by the ancients, called Hecate before and after setting; Astarte when in crescent form; Diana when in full. See Luna.

"Soon as the evening shades prevail
The moon takes up her wondrous tale,
And nightly to the list'ning earth
Repeats the story of her birth."
Addison.

Morpheus (Mor'pheus). The Greek god of sleep and dreams, the son and minister of Somnus.

"Morpheus, the humble god that dwells
In cottages and smoky cells;
Hates gilded roofs and beds of down,
And though he fears no prince's frown,
Flies from the circle of a crown."
Sir John Denman.

Mors. Death, a daughter of Nox (Night).

Mountain, see Atlas, Nymph.

Mulciber (Mul'ciber). A name of Vulcan, sometimes spelled Mulcifer, the smelter of metals. See Vulcan.

Munin (Mun'in). The Scandinavian god of memory, represented by the raven that was perched on Odin's shoulder.

Muscarius (Musca'rius). A name given to Jupiter because he kept off the flies from the sacrifices.

Muses, The (Mu'ses), were nine daughters of Jupiter and Mnemosyne. They presided over the arts and sciences, music and poetry. Their names were, Calliope, Clio, Erato, Thalia, Melpomene, Terpsichore, Euterpe, Polyhymnia, and Urania. They principally resided in Mount Parnassus, at Helicon.

"Be thou the tenth Muse, ten times more in worth,
Than those old nine which rhymers advocate."
Shakespeare.

Music, see Apollo, Muses.

Mythras (My'thras). The Egyptian name of Apollo.

Naiads, The (Nai'ads), were beautiful nymphs of human form who presided over springs, fountains, and wells. They resided in the meadows by the sides of rivers. Virgil mentions Aegle as being the fairest of the Naiades.

Nandi (Nan'di). The Hindoo goddess of joy.

Narrae (Nar'rae). The name of the infernal regions amongst the Hindoos.

Narayan (Na'ra'yan). The mover of the waters. The Hindoo god of tides.

Narcissus (Narcis'sus), son of Cephisus and the Naiad Liriope, was a beautiful youth, who was so pleased with the reflection of himself which he saw in the placid water of a fountain that he could not help loving it, imagining that it must be some beautiful nymph. His fruitless endeavors to possess himself of the supposed nymph drove him to despair, and he killed himself. There sprang from his blood a flower, which was named after him, Narcissus.

"Narcissus so himself forsook,
And died to kiss his shadow in the brook."

"Hadst thou Narcissus in thy face, to me
Thou wouldst appear most ugly."
Shakespeare.

Nastrond (Nas'trond). The Scandinavian place of eternal punishment, corresponding with Hades.

Natio (Na'tio). A Roman goddess who took care of young infants.

Nemaean Lion (Nemae'an), see Hercules.

Nemesis (Nem'esis), the goddess of vengeance or justice, was one of the infernal deities. Her mother was Nox. She was supposed to be constantly traveling about the earth in search of wickedness, which she punished with the greatest severity. She is referred to by some writers under the name of Adrasteia. The Romans always sacrificed to this goddess before they went to war, because they wished to signify that they never took up arms but in the cause of justice.

"Forbear, said Nemesis, my loss to moan,
The fainting, trembling hand was mine alone."
Dr. J. Wharton.

Nephalia (Nepha'lia). Grecian festivals in honor of Mnemosyne, the mother of the Muses.

Neptune (Nep'tune), god of the sea, was a son of Saturn and Cybele, and brother to Jupiter and Pluto. He quarreled with Jupiter because he did not consider that the dominion of the sea was equal to Jupiter's empire of heaven and earth; and he was banished from the celestial regions, after having conspired with Pluto to dethrone Jupiter. Neptune was married to Amphitrite, daughter of Oceanus and Tethys, by whom he had a son named Triton. He was also father of Polyphemus (one of the Cyclopes), Phoreus, and Proteus. Neptune is represented as being seated in a shell chariot, drawn by dolphins or sea-horses, and surrounded by Tritons and sea-nymphs. He holds in his hand a trident, with which he rules the waves. Though a marine deity, he was reputed to have presided over horse-training and horse-races; but he is principally known as the god of the ocean; and the two functions of the god are portrayed in the sea horses with which his chariot is drawn, the fore-half of the animal being a horse, and the hind-half a dolphin. Ships were also under his protection, and whenever he appeared on the ocean there was a dead calm.

Nereides, The (Nere'ides), were aquatic nymphs. They were daughters of Nereus and Doris, and were fifty in number. They are generally represented as beautiful girls riding on dolphins, and carrying tridents in the right hand or garlands of flowers.

Nereus (Nere'us). A sea deity, husband of Doris. He had the gift of prophecy, and foretold fates; but he had also the power of assuming various shapes, which enabled him to escape from the importunities of those who were anxious to consult him.

Nessus (Nes'sus). The name of the Centaur that was destroyed by Hercules for insulting his wife Deianira. Nessus's blood-smeared robe proved fatal to Hercules.

Nestor (Nes'tor). A grandson of Neptune, his father being Neleus, and his mother Chloris. Homer makes him one of the greatest of the Greek heroes. He was present at the famous battle between the Lapithae and the Centaurs, and took a leading part in the Trojan war.

"... Here's Nestor
Instructed by the antiquary times,
He must, he is, he cannot but be wise."
Shakespeare.

Nicephorus (Niceph'orus). A name of Jupiter, meaning the bearer of victory.

Nidhogg (Nid'hogg). In Scandinavian mythology the dragon who dwells in Nastrond.

Niflheim (Nifl'heim). The Scandinavian hell. It was supposed to consist of nine vast regions of ice beneath the North Pole, where darkness reigns eternally. See Nastrond.

Night, see Nox.

Nightingale, see Philomela.

Nightmare, see Incubus.

Nilus (Ni'lus), a king of Thebes, who gave his name to the Nile, the great Egyptian river.

Nine, The, see Muses.

Niobe (Ni'obe) was a daughter of Tantalus, and is the personification of grief. By her husband Amphion she had seven sons and seven daughters. By the orders of Latona the father and sons were killed by Apollo, and the daughters (except Chloris) by Diana. Niobe, being overwhelmed with grief, escaped further trouble by being turned into a stone.

Nomius (No'mius). A law-giver; one of the names of Apollo. This title was also given to Mercury for the part he took in inventing beneficent laws.

Norns. Three Scandinavian goddesses, who wove the woof of human destiny. The three witches in Shakespeare's "Macbeth" have their origin in the Scandinavian Norns.

Notus (No'tus). Another name for Auster, the south wind.

Nox was the daughter of Chaos, and sister of Erebus and Mors. She personified night, and was the mother of Nemesis and the Fates.

Nundina (Nundi'na). The goddess who took charge of children when they were nine days old—the day (Nona dies) on which the Romans named their children.

Nuptialis (Nuptia'lis). A title of Juno. When the goddess was invoked under this name the gall of the victim was taken out and thrown behind the altar, signifying that there should be no gall (bitterness) or anger between married people.

Nuriel (Nu'riel). In Hebrew mythology the god of hailstorms.

Nyctelius (Nycte'lius). A name given to Bacchus, because his festivals were celebrated by torchlight.

Nymphs. This was a general name for a class of inferior female deities who were attendants of the gods. Some of them presided over springs, fountains, wells, woods, and the sea. They are spoken of as land-nymphs or Naiads, and sea-nymphs or Nereids, though the former are associated also with fountains and rivers. The Dryads were forest-nymphs, and the Hamadryads were nymphs who lived among the oak-trees—the oak being always specially venerated by

the ancients. The mountain-nymphs were called Oreads.
"With flower-inwoven tresses torn,
The nymphs in twilight shade
Of tangled thickets mourn."
Milton.

Nysae (Ny'sae). The names of the nymphs by whom Bacchus was nursed. See Dionysius.

Nysaeus (Ny'saeus). A name of Bacchus, because he was worshiped at Nysa, a town of Aethiopia.

Nysus (Ny'sus). A king of Megara who was invisible by virtue of a particular lock of hair. This lock his daughter Scylla cut off, and so betrayed her father to his enemies. She was changed into a lark, and the king into a hawk, and he still pursues his daughter, intending to punish her for her treachery.

Oannes (Oan'nes). An Eastern (Babylonian) god, represented as a monster, half-man, half-fish. He was said to have taught men the use of letters in the day-time, and at night to have retired to the depth of the ocean.

Oath, see Lapis.

Obambou (Obam'bou). A devil of African mythology.

Ocean, see Neptune.

Oceanides (Ocean'ides). Sea-nymphs, daughters of Oceanus and Tethys. Their numbers are variously estimated by different poets; some saying there were as many as 3,000, while others say they were as few as sixteen. The principal of them are mentioned under their respective names, as Amphitrite, Doris, Metis, etc.

Oceanus (Oce'anus), son of Coelus and Terra, and husband of Tethys. Several mythological rivers were called his sons, as Alpheus, Peneus, etc., and his daughters were called the Oceanides. Some of the ancients worshiped him as the god of the seas, and invariably invoked his aid when they were about to start on a voyage. He was also thought to personify the immense stream which it was supposed surrounded the earth, and into which the sun and moon and other heavenly bodies sank every day.

Ocridion (Ocrid'ion). A king of Rhodes, who was deified after his death.

Ocypete (Ocy'pete). One of the Harpies, who infected everything she touched. The word means swift of flight.

Ocyroe (Ocy'roe). A daughter of Chiron, who had the gift of prophecy. She was metamorphosed into a mare.

Odin (O'din). In Scandinavian mythology the god of the universe, and reputed father of all the Scandinavian kings. His wife's name was Friga, and his two sons were Thor and Balder. The Wodin of the early German tribes.

Oeagrus (Oe'agrus). King of Thrace, and father of Orpheus.

Oedipus (Oed'ipus). A son of Laius, King of Thebes, best known as the solver of the famous enigma propounded by the Sphinx. In solving the riddle Oedipus unwittingly killed his father, and, discovering the fact, he destroyed his own eyesight, and wandered away from Thebes, attended by his daughter Antigone. Oedipus is the subject of two famous tragedies by Sophocles.

Oenone (Oeno'ne). Wife of Paris, a nymph of Mount Ida, who had the gift of prophecy.

Ogygia (Ogyg'ia). An island, the abode of Calypso, in the Mediterranean Sea, on which Ulysses was shipwrecked. It was so beautiful in sylvan scenery that even Mercury (who dwelt on Olympus) was charmed with the spot.

Ointment, see Phaon.

Olenus (Ole'nus). A son of Vulcan, who married Lathaea, a woman who thought herself more beautiful than the goddesses, and as a punishment she and her husband were turned into stone statues.

Olives, see Aristaeus.

Olympius (Olym'pius). A name of Jupiter, from Olympia, where the god had a splendid temple, which was considered to be one of the seven wonders of the world.

Olympus (Olym'pus) was the magnificent mountain on the coast of

Thessaly, 9,000 feet high, where the gods were supposed to reside. There were several other smaller mountains of the same name.
"High heaven with trembling the dread signal took,
And all Olympus to the center shook."
Pope.

Olyras (Oly'ras). A river near Thermopylae, which, it is said, attempted to extinguish the funeral pile on which Hercules was consumed.
Omophagia (Omopha'gia). A Bacchanalian festival at which some uncooked meats were served.
Omphale (Om'phale). The Queen of Lydia, to whom Hercules was sold as a bondsman for three years for the murder of Iphitus. Hercules fell in love with her, and led an effeminate life in her society, wearing female apparel, while Omphale wore the lion's skin.
Onarus (Ona'rus). A priest of Bacchus, said to have married Ariadne after she had been abandoned by Theseus.
Onuva (Onu'va). The Venus of the ancient Gauls.
Opalia (Opa'lia). Roman festivals in honor of Ops, held on 14th of the calends of January.
Opiate-rod, see Caduceus.
"Eyes ... more wakeful than to drowse,
Charmed with Arcadian pipe—the pastoral reed
Of Hermes or his opiate-rod."
Milton.

Ops. Mother of the gods, a daughter of Coelus and Terra. She was known by the several names of Bona Dea, Rhea, Cybele, Magna Mater, Proserpine, Tellus, and Thya; and occasionally she is spoken of as Juno and Minerva. She personified labor, and is represented as a comely matron, distributing gifts with her right hand, and holding in her left hand a loaf of bread. Her festival was the 14th day of the

January calends.

Oracles, see Themis.

Oraea (Orae′a). Certain sacrifices offered to the goddesses of the seasons to invoke fair weather for the ripening of the fruits of the earth.

Orbona (Orbo′na). Roman goddess of children, invoked by mothers
when they lost or were in danger of losing their offspring.

Orchards, see Feronia.

Oreades (O′reades) were mountain nymphs, attendants on Diana.

Orgies. Drunken revels. The riotous feasts of Bacchus were so desi-
gnated.

Orion (Ori′on). A handsome hunter, of great stature, who was blin-
ded by Oenopion for a grievous wrong done to Merope, and was
therefore expelled from Chios. The sound of the Cyclops' hammers
led him to the abode of Vulcan, who gave him a guide. He then con-
sulted an oracle, and had his sight restored, as Longfellow says, by fi-
xing

"His blank eyes upon the sun."

He was afterward slain by Diana and placed amongst the stars, where his constellation is one of the most splendid.

Orithyia (Ori′thy′ia). A daughter of Erechtheus, whose lover, Boreas,
carried her off while she was wandering by the river Ilissus. Her children were Zetus and Calais, two winged warriors who accompanied
the Argonauts.

Ormuzd (Or′muzd). In Persian mythology the creator of all things.

Oros (O′ros). The Egyptian Apollo.

Orphans, see Orbona.

Orpheus (Or′pheus) was son of Apollo and the Muse Calliope. He
was married to Eurydice; but she was stung by a serpent, and died.
Orpheus went down to Hades to claim her, and played so sweetly
with his lute that Pluto allowed Eurydice to return to the earth with
Orpheus, but on condition that he did not look behind him until he

had reached the terrestrial regions. Orpheus, however, in his anxiety to see if she were following him, looked round, and Eurydice disappeared from his sight, instantly and forever.
"Orpheus' lute was strung with poets' sinews."
Shakespeare.

Osiris (Osi´ris). The Egyptian god of the sun, the source of warmth, life, and fruitfulness; he was worshiped under the form of a sacred bull, named Apis.
"... After these appeared
A crew who, under names of old renown,
Osiris, Isis, Orus, and their train,
With monstrous shapes and sorceries abused
Fanatic Egypt and her priests to seek
Their wandering gods, disguised in brutish forms
Rather than human."
Milton.

Ossa (Os´sa). One of the mountains of Thessaly (once the residence of the centaurs) which the giants piled on the top of Mount Pelion to enable them to ascend to heaven and attack the gods.
Ox, see Apis.
Owl, see Aesculapius and Itys.
Pactolus (Pacto´lus). The river in Lydia where Midas washed himself by order of Bacchus, and the sands were turned to gold.
Paean (Pae´an). A name given Apollo, from paean, the hymn which was sung in his honor after he had killed the serpent Python. Paeans were solemn songs, praying either for the averting of evil and for rescue, or giving thanks for help vouchsafed.
"With hymns divine the joyous banquet ends,
The Paeans lengthened till the sun descends."

Pope.

Palaemon (Palae'mon), or Melicerta, a sea-god, son of Athamas and
Ino.
Pales (Pa'les). The goddess of shepherds and sheepfolds and protec-
tress of flocks; her festivals were called by the Romans Palilia.
"Pomona loves the orchard,
And Liber loves the wine,
And Pales loves the straw-built shed,
Warm with the breath of kine."
Macaulay.

"Great Pales help, the pastoral rites I sing,
With humble duty mentioning each thing."
Pope.

Palladium (Palla'dium). A famous statue of the goddess Pallas (Minerva). She is sitting with a spear in her right hand, and in her left a
distaff and spindle. Various accounts are given of the origin of the
statue. Some writers say that it fell from the skies. It was supposed
that the preservation of the statue would be the preservation of
Troy; and during the Trojan War the Greeks were greatly encoura-
ged when they became the possessors of it.
Pallas (Pal'las), or Minerva. The name was given to Minerva when
she destroyed a famous giant named Pallas. The Greeks called their
goddess of wisdom Pallas Athene. See Minerva.
"Apollo, Pallas, Jove, or Mercury,
Inspire me that I may this treason find."

Shakespeare.

Iris

Pan. The Arcadian god of shepherds, huntsmen, and country folk,
and chief of the inferior deities, is usually considered to have been
the son of Mercury and Penelope. After his birth he was metamorphosed into the mythical form in which we find him depicted, na-
mely, a horned, long-eared man, with the lower half of the body like
a goat. He is generally seen playing a pipe made of reeds of various
lengths, which he invented himself, and from which he could produce music which charmed even the gods. These are the Pan-pipes, or
Syrinx. Pan's terrific appearance once so frightened the Gauls when
they invaded Greece that they ran away though no one pursued
them; and the word panic is said to have been derived from this epi-

sode. The Fauns, who greatly resembled Pan, were his attendants.

"Piping on their reeds the shepherds go,
Nor fear an ambush, nor suspect a foe."
Pope.

Pandora (Pando'ra), according to Hesiod, was the first mortal female. Vulcan made her of clay, and gave her life. Venus gave her beauty; and the art of captivating was bestowed upon her by the Graces.
She was taught singing by Apollo, and Mercury taught her oratory.
Jupiter gave her a box, the famous "Pandora's Box," which she was
told to give to her husband, Epimetheus, brother of Prometheus. As
soon as he opened it there issued from it numberless diseases and
evils which were soon spread all over the world, and from that moment they have afflicted the human race. It is said that Hope alone
remained in the box. Pandora means "the all-gifted."
"More lovely than Pandora, whom the gods
Endowed with all their gifts."
Milton.

Pantheon (Panthe'on) (lit. "the all-divine place"). The temple of all
the gods, built by Agrippa at Rome, in the reign of Augustus (B.C.
27). It was 144 feet in diameter, and 144 feet high; and was built in the
Corinthian style of architecture, mostly of marble; while its walls
were covered with engraved brass and silver. Its magnificence indu-
ced Pliny to give it rank among the wonders of the world.
Paphia (Pa'phia), a name of Venus.
Papremis (Pap'remis). The Egyptian Mars.
Parcae, The (Par'cae), were goddesses who presided over the destiny

of human beings. They were also called the Fates, and were three in number, Atropos, Clotho, and Lachesis. See Fates.

Paris (Par′is), the son of Priam, king of Troy, and of his mother Hecuba. It had been predicted that he would be the cause of the destruction of Troy, and his father therefore ordered him to be strangled as soon as he was born; but the slave who had been entrusted with this mission took the child to Mount Ida, and left it there. Some shepherds, however, found the infant and took care of him. He lived among them till he had grown to man's estate, and he then married Oenone, a nymph of Ida. At the famous nuptial feast of Peleus and Thetis, Discordia, who had not been invited, attended secretly; and when all were assembled, she threw among the goddesses a golden apple, on which was inscribed "Let the fairest take it." This occasioned a great contention, for each thought herself the fairest. Ultimately, the contestants were reduced to three, Juno, Pallas (Minerva), and Venus; but Jove himself could not make these three agree, and it was decided that Paris should be the umpire. He was sent for, and each of the goddesses courted his favor by offering all sorts of bribes. Juno offered him power, Pallas wisdom, and Venus promised him the most beautiful woman in the world. Paris gave the golden apple to Venus. Soon after this episode Priam owned Paris as his son, and sent him to Greece to fetch Helen, who was renowned as being the most beautiful woman in the world. She was the wife of Menelaus, king of Sparta; but during his absence Paris carried Helen away to Troy, and this gave rise to the celebrated war between the Greeks and the Trojans, which ended in the destruction of Troy. Paris was among the 676,000 Trojans who fell during or after the siege.

Parnassides (Parnas′sides), a name common to the Muses, from Mount Parnassus.

Parnassus (Parnas′sus). The mountain of the Muses in Phocis, and sacred to Apollo and Bacchus. Any one who slept on this mountain became a poet. It was named after one of the sons of Bacchus.

Parthenon (Par′thenon). The temple of Minerva (or Pallas) on the Acropolis at Athens. It was destroyed by the Persians, and rebuilt by

Pericles.

Parthenos (Par′thenos) was a name of Juno, and also of Minerva. See Pallas.

Pasiphae (Pasiph′ae) was the reputed mother of the Minotaur killed by Theseus. She was said to be the daughter of Sol and Perseis, and her husband was Minos, king of Crete.

Pasithea (Pasith′ea). Sometimes there are four Graces spoken of; when this is so, the name of the fourth is Pasithea. Also called Aglaia.

Pavan (Pav′an), the Hindoo god of the winds.

Peace, see Concordia.

Peacock, see Argus.

Pegasus (Peg′asus). The famous winged horse which was said to have sprung from the blood of Medusa when her head was cut off by Perseus. His abode was on Mount Helicon, where, by striking the ground with his hoof, he caused water to spring forth, which formed the fountain afterward called Hippocrene.

"Each spurs his faded
Pegasus apace."
Byron.

"Thy stumbling founder'd jade can trot as high
As any other Pegasus can fly."
Earl of Dorset.

"To turn and wind a fiery Pegasus,
And witch the world with noble horsemanship."
Shakespeare.

Peleus (Pe′leus). A king of Thessaly, who married Thetis, one of the

Nereides. It is said that he was the only mortal who married an immortal.

Pelias (Pe'lias). A son of Neptune and Tyro. He usurped the throne of Cretheus, which Jason was persuaded to relinquish and take the command of the Argonautic expedition. On the return of Jason, Medea, the sorceress, undertook to restore Pelias to youth, but required that the body should first be cut up and put in a caldron of boiling water. When this had been done, Medea refused to fulfil her promise. Pelias had four daughters, who were called the Peliades.

Pelias (Pe'lias) was the name of the spear of Achilles, which was so large that none could wield it but the hero himself.

Pelion (Pe'lion). A well-wooded mountain, famous for the wars between the giants and the gods, and as the abode of the Centaurs, who were expelled by the Lapithae. See Ossa, a mount, which the giants piled upon Pelion, to enable them to scale the heavens.

"The gods they challenge, and affect the skies,
Heaved on Olympus tottering Ossa stood;
On Ossa, Pelion nods with all his wood."
Pope.

Pelops (Pe'lops), son of Tantalus, king of Phrygia. His father killed him, and served him up to be eaten at a feast given to the gods, who, when they found out what the father of Pelops had done, restored the son to life, and he afterward became the husband of Hippodamia.

Penates (Pena'tes). Roman domestic gods. The hearth of the house was their altar. See Lares.

Perpetual Punishment, see Sisyphus.

Persephone (Perseph'one). The Greek name of Proserpine.

Perseus (Per'seus) was a son of Jupiter and Danae, the daughter of Acrisius. His first famous exploit was against the Gorgon, Medusa. He was assisted in this enterprise by Pluto, who lent him a helmet which would make him invisible. Pallas lent him her shield, and Mercury supplied him with wings. He made a speedy conquest of the Gorgons, and cut off Medusa's head, with which he flew through the air, and from the blood sprang the winged horse Pegasus. As he flew along he saw Andromeda chained to the rock, and a sea-monster ready to devour her. He killed the monster, and married Andromeda. When he got back, he showed the Gorgon's head to King Polydectes, and the monarch was immediately turned into stone.

"Now on Daedalian waxen pinions stray,
Or those which wafted Perseus on his way."
F. Lewis.

Persuasion, goddess of, see Pitho.

Phaeton (Pha'eton). A son of Sol, or, according to many mythologists, of Phoebus and Clymene. Anxious to display his skill in horsemanship, he was allowed to drive the chariot of the sun for one day. The horses soon found out the incapacity of the charioteer, became unmanageable, and overturned the chariot. There was such great fear of injury to heaven and earth, that Jove, to stop the destruction, killed Phaeton with a thunderbolt.

"Now Phaeton, by lofty hopes possessed,
The burning seat with youthful vigor pressed."

"The breathless Phaeton, with flaming hair,
Shot from the chariot like a falling star
That in a summer's evening from the top
Of heaven drops down, or seems at least to drop."
Addison.

Phaon (Pha'on). A boatman of Mitylene, in Lesbos, who received from Venus a box of ointment, with which, when he anointed himself, he grew so beautiful that Sappho became enamored of him; but when the ointment had all been used Phaon returned to his former condition, and Sappho, in despair, drowned herself.

Pheasant, see Itys.

Philoctetes (Philoct'etes) was son of Poeas, and one of the companions of Jason on his Argonautic expedition. He was present at the death of Hercules, and received from him the poisoned arrows which had been dipped in the blood of Hydra. These arrows, an oracle declared, were necessary to be used in the destruction of Troy, and Philoctetes was persuaded by Ulysses to go and assist at the siege. He appears to have used the weapons with great dexterity and with wonderful effect, for Paris was among the heroes whom he killed. The story of Philoctetes was dramatized by the Greek tragedians Aeschylus, Euripides, and Sophocles.

Philomela (Philome'la) was a daughter of Pandion, king of Athens, who was transformed into a nightingale. She was sister to Procne, who married Tereus, King of Thrace. The latter having offered violence to Philomela, her sister, Procne, came to her rescue, and to punish her husband slew her son Itylus, and at a feast Philomela threw Itylus's head on the banquet table.

"Forth like a fury Philomela flew,
And at his face the head of Itys threw."
Pope.

"And thou, melodious Philomel,
Again thy plaintive story tell."
Sir Thomas Lyttleton.

Phlegethon (Phleg'ethon). A river of fire in the infernal regions. It was the picture of desolation, for nothing could grow on its parched and withered banks. Also called Pyriphlegethon.
"... Infernal rivers ...
... Fierce Phlegethon,
Whose waves of torrent fire inflame with rage."
Milton.

Phlegon (Phle'gon) (burning), one of the four chariot horses of Sol.
Phlegyas (Phle'gyas). Son of Mars and father of Ixion and Coronis. For his impiety in desecrating and plundering the temple of Apollo at Delphi, he was sent to Hades, and there was made to sit with a huge stone suspended over his head, ready to be dropped on him at any moment.
Phoebus (Phoe'bus). A name of Apollo, signifying light and life.
"Gallop apace, you fiery-footed steeds,
Toward Phoebus' lodging."
Shakespeare.

Phorcus (Phor'cus), or Porcys. A son of Neptune, father of the Gorgons. The same as Oceanus.
Phryxus (Phryx'us), see Golden Fleece.
Picumnus (Picum'nus). A rural divinity, who presided over the manuring of lands, also called Sterentius.
Picus (Pi'cus). A son of Saturn, father of Faunus, was turned into a woodpecker by Circe, whose love he had not requited.
Pierides (Pier'ides). A name of the Muses, derived from Pieria, a fountain in Thessaly, near Mount Olympus, where they were supposed to have been born. Also, the daughters of Pierus, a king of Macedonia, who settled in Boeotia. They challenged the Muses to sing, and were changed into magpies.

Pietas (Pie′tas). The Roman goddess of domestic affection.

Pillar, see Calpe.

Pilumnus (Pilum′nus). A rural divinity that presided over the corn while it was being ground. At Rome he was hence called the god of bakers.

Pine-Tree, see Atys.

Pirithous (Pirith′ous). A son of Ixion and great friend of Theseus, king of Athens. The marriage of Pirithous and Hippodamia became famous for the quarrel between the drunken Centaurs and the Lapithae, who, with the help of Theseus, Pirithous, and Hercules, attacked and overcame the Centaurs, many of whom were killed, and the remainder took to flight.

Pitho (Pi′tho), the goddess of Persuasion, daughter of Mercury and Venus. She is sometimes referred to under the name of Suada.

Plants, see Demogorgon.

Pleasure, see Rembha.

Pleiades, The (Plei′ades). Seven daughters of Atlas and Pleione. Their names were Electra, Alcyone, Celaeno, Maia, Sterope, Taygete, and Merope. They were made a constellation, but as there are only six stars to be seen, the ancients believed that one of the sisters, Merope, married a mortal, and was ashamed to show herself among her sisters, who had all been married to gods.

"... The gray
Dawn and the Pleiades before him danced.
Shedding sweet influence."
Milton.

Pluto (Plu′to). King of the infernal regions. He was a son of Saturn and Ops, and husband of Proserpine, daughter of Ceres. He is sometimes referred to under the name Dis, and he personifies hell. His principal attendant was the three-headed dog Cerberus, and about his throne were the Eumenides, the Harpies, and the Furies.

"With equal foot, rich friend, impartial fate
Knocks at the cottage and the palace gate.

. . . . .

Night soon will seize, and you must go below,
To story'd ghosts and Pluto's house below."
Creech.

Plutus (Plu'tus), the god of riches, was son of Jasion or Iasius and Ceres (Demeter), the goddess of corn. He is described as being blind and lame; blind because he so often injudiciously bestows his riches, and lame because fortunes come so slowly.

Pluvius (Plu'vius). A name of Jupiter, because he had the rain in his control.

Podalirius (Podalir'ius). A famous surgeon, a son of Aesculapius and Epione. His skill in medicine made him very serviceable among the soldiers in the Trojan war.

Poet, see Parnassus.

Poetry, see Apollo, Calliope, The Muses.

Poisonous Herbs, see Circe.

Poisonous Lake, see Avernus.

Pollear (Poll'ear). Son of Siva, the Hindoo god of wisdom.

Pollux (Pol'lux). Twin brother of Castor. Their father was Jupiter and their mother Leda. He and his brother form the constellation Gemini. His Greek name was Polydeuces. Castor and Pollux are also known under the name of Dioscuri, the presiding deities of public games in Rome, Castor being the god of equestrian exercise, and Pollux the god of boxing. See Aedepol.

Polybotes (Polybo'tes). One of the giants who made war against Jupiter. He was killed by Neptune.

Polydectes (Polydec'tes) was turned into stone when Perseus showed him Medusa's head. See Perseus.

Polydeuces (Polydeu'ces). The Greek name of Pollux.

Polyhymnia (Polyhym'nia). Daughter of Jupiter and Mnemosyne.

One of the Muses who presided over singing and rhetoric.

Polyphemus (Polyphe′mus), one of the most celebrated of the Cyclops, a son of the nymph Thoosa and Neptune, or Poseidon, as the
Greeks called the god of the sea. He captured Ulysses and twelve of
his companions, and it is said that six of them were eaten. The remainder escaped by the ingenuity of Ulysses, who destroyed Polyphemus's one eye with a fire-brand.

"Charybdis barks and Polyphemus roars."

Francis.

Polyxena (Polyx′ena). Daughter of Hecuba and Priam, king of Troy.
It was by her treachery that Achilles was shot in the heel.

Laocoon

Pomona (Pomo′na). The Roman goddess of fruit-trees and gardens.

"So to the sylvan lodge
They came, that like Pomona's arbor smiled
With flowerets decked and fragrant smells."
Milton.

Poplar-Tree, see Heliades.
Portunus (Portu'nus) (Palaemon), son of Ino, was the Roman god of harbors.
Poseidon (Posei'don). The Greek name of Neptune, god of the sea.
Pracriti (Prac'riti). The Hindoo goddess of nature.
Predictions, see Cassandra.
Priam (Pri'am). The last king of Troy. See Paris.
Priapus (Pria'pus), the guardian of gardens and god of natural reproduction, was the son of Venus and Bacchus.
"Priapus could not half describe the grace
(Though god of gardens) of this charming place."
Pope.

Prisca (Pris'ca). Another name of Vesta.
Procris (Pro'cris). Daughter of Erechtheus, king of Athens. See Cephalus, her husband.
Progne (Prog'ne), wife of Tereus. Commonly called Procne, whose sister was Philomela. See Itys and Tereus.
"Complaining oft gives respite to our grief,
From hence the wretched Progne sought relief."
F. Lewis.

Prometheus (Prome'theus), the son of Japetus and father of Deucalion. He presumed to make clay men, and animate them with fire which he had stolen from heaven. This so displeased Jupiter that he sent him a box full of evils, which Prometheus refused; but his brother Epimetheus, not so cautious, opened it, and the evils spread over all the earth. Jupiter then punished Prometheus by commanding Mercury to bind him to Mount Caucasus, where a vulture daily preyed upon his liver, which grew in the night as much as it had been reduced in the day, so that the punishment was a prolonged torture. Hercules at last killed the vulture and set Prometheus free.

Prophecy, see Nereus.

Proserpine (Proser'pine). A daughter of Jupiter and Ceres. Pluto carried her off to the infernal regions and made her his wife. She was known by the names of "the Queen of Hell," Hecate, Juno Inferna, and Libitina. She was called by the Greeks Persephone.

"He sung, and hell consented
To hear the poet's prayer,
Stern Proserpine relented,
And gave him back the fair."
F. Lewis.

Proteus (Pro'teus). A marine deity, who could foretell events and convert himself at will into all sorts of shapes. According to later legends, Proteus was a son of Poseidon.

"The changeful Protcus, whose prophetic mind,
The secret cause of Bacchus' rage divined."
The Lusiad.

"What chain can hold this varying Proteus fast?"
Budgell.

Psyche (Psy'che). The wife of Cupid. The name is Greek, signifying the soul or spirit.

Pygmalion (Pygma'lion). A famous sculptor who had resolved to remain unmarried, but he made such a beautiful statue of a goddess that he begged Venus to give it life. His request being granted, Pygmalion married the animated statue.

"Few, like Pygmalion, doat on lifeless charms,
Or care to clasp a statue in their arms."

Pylades (Py'lades). The son of Strophius, King of Phanote, and husband of Electra; famous on account of his faithful friendship with Orestes.

"His wine
Was better, Pylades, than thine.
... If you please
To choose me for your Pylades."
F. Lewis.

Pylotis (Pylo'tis). A Greek name of Minerva.

Pyracmon (Pyr'acmon), one of the chiefs of the Cyclopes.

Pyramus and Thisbe (Pyr'amus and This'be). Two Babylonian lovers, the children of hostile neighbors. See Shakespeare's burlesque of the story of their loves, in "Midsummer Night's Dream."

Pyrois (Py'rois) (luminous). One of the four chariot horses of Sol, the Sun.

Pythia (Py'thia). The priestess of Apollo at Delphi, who delivered the answers of the oracle. Also the name of the Pythian games celebrated in honor of Apollo's victory over the dragon Python.

Python (Py'thon). A famous serpent killed by Apollo, which haunted the caves of Parnassus. See Septerion.

Quadratus (Quadra′tus). A surname given to Mercury, because some of his statues were four-sided.

Quadrifrons (Quad′rifrons). Janus was sometimes depicted with four faces instead of the usual two, and he was then called Janus Quadrifrons.

Quies (Qui′es). The Roman goddess of rest; she had a temple just outside the Colline gate of Rome.

Quietus (Quie′tus). One of the names of Pluto.

Quirinus (Quiri′nus). A name given to Mars during wartime; Virgil refers to Jupiter under the same name.

Quoit, see Hyacinthus.

Race, see Atalanta.

Radamanthus (Radaman′thus), see Rhadamanthus.

Rage, see Furies.

Rainbow, see Iris.

Rama (Ra′ma). A Hindoo god, who was the terrestrial representative of Vishnu.

Ram's Hide, see Golden Fleece.

Reeds, see Pan, also Syrinx.

Rembha (Rem′bha). The Hindoo goddess of pleasure.

Reproduction, see Priapus.

Rest, see Quies.

Revenge, see Ate.

Rhadamanthus (Rhadaman′thus), a son of Jupiter and Europa, was the ruler of the Greeks in the Asiatic islands, and judge of the dead in the infernal regions.

"These are the realms of unrelenting fate:
And awful Rhadamanthus rules the state.
He hears and judges each committed crime,
Inquires into the manner, place, and time;
The conscious wretch must all his acts reveal,
Loth to confess, unable to conceal;
From the first moment of his vital breath,
To the last hour of unrepenting death."

Dryden.

Rhamnusia (Rhamnu'sia). A name of Nemesis, from Rhamnus, a town in Attica, where she had a temple in which was her statue, made of one stone ten cubits high.

Rhea (Rhe'a). The Greek name of Cybele. She was a daughter of Uranus and Gaea, and was called Mother of the gods.

Rhetoric, see Calliope, also Polyhymnia.

Riches, see Plutus.

Riddle, see Sphinx.

Rimmon (Rim'mon). A Phrygian god of whom Milton says—

"... Rimmon, whose delightful seat

Was fair Damascus, on the fertile banks

Of Abana and Pharpar, lucid streams."

Riot, see Saturnalia.

River of Fire, see Phlegethon.

Roads, see Vialis.

Robber, see Cacus, Coeculus.

Romulus (Rom'ulus). The traditional founder of Rome. He was a son of Mars and Ilia, and twin brother of Remus. The infants were thrown into the Tiber, but were miraculously saved and suckled by a she-wolf, till they were found by Faustulus, a shepherd, who brought them up. Remus was killed in a quarrel with his brother, and Romulus became the first King of Rome.

Rumia Dea (Rumi'a Dea). The Roman goddess of babes in arms.

Rumina (Ru'mina). Roman pastoral deities, who protected suckling cattle.

Runcina (Runci'na). The goddess of weeding or cleansing the ground.

Sacrifices were ceremonious offerings made to the gods. To every deity a distinct victim was allotted, and the greatest care was always taken in the selection of them. Anything in any way blemished was considered as an insult to the god. At the time of the sacrifice the people were called together by heralds led by a procession of musicians. The priest, clothed in white, was crowned with a wreath made of the leaves of the tree which was sacred to the particular god to whom the sacrifice was offered. The victim had its horns gilt, and was adorned with a chaplet similar to that of the priest, and was decorated with bright-colored ribbons. The priest then said, "Who is here?" to which the spectators replied, "Many good people." "Begone all ye who are profane," said the priest; and he then began a prayer addressed to all the gods. The sacrifice was begun by putting corn, frankincense, flour, salt, cakes, and fruit on the head of the victim. This was called the Immolation. The priest then took a cup of wine, tasted it, and handed it to the bystanders to taste also; some of it was then poured between the horns of the victim, and a few of the saturated hairs were pulled off and put in the fire which was burning on the altar. Then, turning to the east, the priest drew with his knife a crooked line along the back of the beast from the head to the tail, and told the assistants to kill the animal. This was done directly, and the entrails of the victim taken out and carefully examined by the Haruspices to find out what was prognosticated. The carcase was then divided, and the thighs, covered with fat, were put in the fire, and the rest of the animal was cut up, cooked, and eaten. This feast was celebrated with dancing, music, and hymns, in praise of the god in whose honor the sacrifice was made. On great occasions as many as a hundred bullocks were offered at one time; and it is said that Pythagoras made this offering when he found out the demonstration of the forty-seventh proposition of the book of Euclid.

Saga (Sa'ga). The Scandinavian goddess of history. The word means a saw or saying; hence Sagas, which embody Scandinavian legends, and heroic or mythical traditions.

Sagittarius (Sagitta'rius), see Chiron.

Sails, see Daedalus.

Salamanders (Sal'aman'ders). The genii who, according to Plato, li-
ved in fire.
"The spirits of fiery termagants in flame,
Mount up and take a Salamander's name."
Pope.

Salatia (Sala'tia), or Salacia, a Roman goddess of the salt water. See
Amphitrite.
Salii (Sal'ii). The priests of Mars who had charge of the sacred
shields.
Salmoneus (Salmo'neus). A king of Elis who, for trying to imitate Ju-
piter's thunders, was sent by the god straight to the infernal regions.
Salus (Sa'lus). The Roman goddess of health.
Sappho (Sap'pho), a celebrated poetess, a native of Lesbos, who flou-
rished in the seventh century B.C. Her only connection with the
goddesses of the time is that the Greeks called her "The tenth Muse."
Sarcasm, see Momus.
Saron (Sa'ron), a sea-god.
Sarpedon (Sarpe'don), son of Jupiter by Europa. He accompanied
Glaucus, when the latter set out to assist Priam against the Greeks in
the Trojan War. He was slain by Patroclus.
Saturn (Sat'urn), king of the Universe, was father of Jupiter, Neptune, and Pluto. These gods quarreled amongst themselves as to the
division of their father's kingdom, which ended in Jupiter having
heaven and earth, Neptune the sea, and Pluto the infernal regions.
Saturnalia (Saturna'lia). Festivals held in honor of Saturn about the
16th or 18th of December. Principally famous for the riotous disor-
der which generally attended them.
Saturnius (Satur'nius). A name given to Jupiter, Neptune, and Pluto,
as sons of Saturn.
Satyavrata (Satya'vra'ta). The Hindoo god of law. The same as Menu.
Satyrs (Sat'yrs). Spirits of the woodland, half men, half goats, and
fond of wine and women. They were the attendants of Dionysus,

and were similar in most respects to the fauns who attended Pan.
See Silenus.
"Five satyrs of the woodland sort.

. . . . . .
With asses' hoofs, great goggle eyes,
And double chins of monstrous size."
Yalden.

Scylla (Scyl'la). A beautiful nymph who excited the jealousy of Neptune's wife, Amphitrite, and was changed by the goddess into a frightful sea-monster, which had six fearfully ugly heads and necks, and which, rising unexpectedly from the deep, used to take off as many as six sailors from a vessel, and carry them to the bottom of the sea. An alternative danger with the whirlpool, Charybdis, which threatened destruction to all mariners.
"There on the right her dogs foul Scylla hides,
Charybdis roaring on the left presides."
Virgil.

Scylla (Scyl'la). A daughter of Nysus, who was changed into a lark for cutting off a charmed lock of her father's hair. See Nysus.
Sea, see Neptune.
Seasons, see Vertumnus.
Sea-Weed, see Glaucus.
Segetia (Sege'tia). A rural divinity who protected corn during harvest-time.
Sem. The Egyptian Hercules.
Semele (Sem'ele), daughter of Cadmus and the mother of Bacchus (Dionysus), who was born in a miraculous manner after Jupiter had visited her, at her special request, in all his terrible splendor. She was

deified after her death, and named Thyone.

Semi-Dei were the demi-gods.

Semones (Semo'nes). Roman gods of a class between the "immortal" and the "mortal," such as the Satyrs and Fauns.

Septerion (Septe'rion). A festival held every nine years at Delphi in honor of Apollo, at which the victory of that god over the Python was grandly represented.

Serapis (Sera'pis). The Egyptian Jupiter, and generally considered to be the same as Osiris. See Apis.

Serpent. The Greeks and Romans considered the serpent as symbolical of guardian spirits, and as such were often engraved on their altars. See Aesculapius, Apollo, Chimaera, Eurydice, and Medusa.

"Pleasing was his shape,

And lovely; never since of serpent kind,

Lovelier; not those that in Illyria changed

Hermione and Cadmus, or the god

In Epidaurus, nor to which transformed

Ammonian Jove, or Capitoline, was seen."

Milton.

Seshanaga (Sesh'anag'a). The Egyptian Pluto.

Sewers, see Cloacina.

Sharp-sightedness, see Lynceus.

Shepherds, see Pan.

Shields, see Ancilia.

Ships, see Neptune.

Silence, see Harpocrates and Tacita.

Silenus (Sile'nus). A Bacchanalian demi-god, the chief of the Satyrs. He is generally represented as a fat, drunken old man, riding on an ass, and crowned with flowers.

"And there two Satyrs on the ground,

Stretched at his ease, their sire Silenus found."

Singing, see Polyhymnia, Thamyris.

Sirens, The (Si'rens). Sea nymphs, who by their music allured mariners to destruction. To avoid the snare when nearing their abode, Ulysses had the ears of his companions stopped with wax, and had himself tied to the mast of his ship. They thus sailed past in safety; but the Sirens, thinking that their charms had lost their powers, drowned themselves.

Sisyphus (Sis'yphus), son of Aeolus and Enaretta. He was condemned to roll a stone to the top of a hill in the infernal regions, and as it rolled down again when he reached the summit, his punishment was perpetual.

"I turned my eye, and as I turned, surveyed
A mournful vision! The Sisyphian shade.
With many a weary step and many a groan,
Up the high hill he leaves a huge round stone,
The huge round stone, resulting with a bound
Thunders impetuous down, and smokes along the ground."
Pope.

"Thy stone, O Sisyphus, stands still
Ixion rests upon his wheel,
And the pale specters dance."
F. Lewis.

Siva (Si'va). In Hindoo mythology the "changer of form." He is usually spoken of as the "Destroyer and Regenerator."

Slaughter, see Furies.

Slaves, see Feronia.

Sleep, see Caduceus, Morpheus, and Somnus.
Sleipner (Sleip′ner). The eight-legged horse of Odin, the chief of the Scandinavian gods.

Winged Mercury

Sol. The sun. The worship of the god Sol is the oldest on record, and though he is sometimes referred to as being the same as the god Apollo, there is no doubt he was worshiped by the Egyptians, Persians, and other nations long before the Apollo of the Greeks was heard of. See Surya.
"Sol through white curtains shot a timorous ray,
And oped those eyes that must eclipse the day."
Pope.

Somnus (Som′nus). The Roman god of sleep, son of Erebus and Nox

(Night). He was one of the infernal deities, and resided in a gloomy cave, void of light and air.

Sospita (Sos′pita). A name of Juno, as the safeguard of women. She is called the "saving goddess."

Soter (So′ter). A Greek name of Jupiter, meaning Savior or deliverer.

Soul, see Psyche.

South Wind, see Auster.

Spear, see Pelias.

Sphinx, The. A monster having the head and breast of a woman, the body of a dog, the tail of a serpent, the wings of a bird, the paws of a lion, and a human voice. She lived in the country near Thebes, and proposed to every passer-by the following enigma: "What animal is that which walks on four legs in the morning, two at noon, and three in the evening." Oedipus solved the riddle thus: Man is the animal; for, when an infant he crawls on his hands and feet, in the noontide of life he walks erect, and as the evening of his existence sets in, he supports himself with a stick. When the Sphinx found her riddle solved she destroyed herself.

Spider, see Arachne.

Spindle, see Pallas.

Spinning, see Arachne, Ergatis.

Spring, see Vertumnus.

Stable, see Augaeas.

Stars, see Aurora.

Sterentius (Steren′tius). The Roman god who invented the art of manuring lands. See also Picumnus.

Steropes (Ster′opes). One of the Cyclopes.

Stone, see Medusa and Phlegyas.

Stone (rolling), see Sisyphus.

Streets, see Apollo.

Stymphalides (Stym′phali′des). The carnivorous birds destroyed in the sixth labor of Hercules.

Styx. A noted river of hell, which was held in such high esteem by the gods that they always swore "By the Styx," and such an oath was never violated. The river has to be crossed in passing to the regions of the dead. See Achilles and Thetis.

"To seal his sacred vow by Styx he swore:—
The lake with liquid pitch,—the dreary shore."
Dryden.

"... Infernal rivers that disgorge
Into the burning lake their baleful streams,
Abhorrèd Styx, the flood of deadly hate."

Suada (Sua'da), the goddess of Persuasion. See Pitho.
Success, see Bonus Eventus.
Sun, see Aurora, Belus, Sol, and Surya.
Sunflower, see Clytie.
Suradevi (Sura'de'vi). The Hindoo goddess of wine.
Surgeon (Sur'geon), see Podalirius.
Surya (Su'ry'a). The Hindoo god corresponding to the Roman Sol, the sun.
Swallow, see Itys.
Swan, see Cygnus and Leda.
Swiftness, see Atalanta.
Swine, see Circe.
Sylphs. Genii who, according to Plato, lived in the air.
"The light coquettes as Sylphs aloft repair,
And sport and flutter in the fields of air."
Pope.

Sylvester (Sylves'ter). The name of Mars when he was invoked to protect cultivated land from the ravages of war.

Syrinx. The name of the nymph who, to escape from the importunities of Pan, was by Diana changed into reeds, out of which he made his celebrated pipes, and named them "The Syrinx."

Tacita (Tac'ita). The goddess of Silence. See Harpocrates, also Horus.

Tantalus (Tan'talus). Father of Niobe and Pelops, who, as a punishment for serving up his son Pelops as meat at a feast given to the gods, was placed in a pool of water in the infernal regions; but the waters receded from him whenever he attempted to quench his burning thirst. Hence the word "tantalizing".

Speaking of this god, Homer's Ulysses says: "I saw the severe punishment of Tantalus. In a lake, whose waters approached to his lips, he stood burning with thirst, without the power to drink. Whenever he inclined his head to the stream, some deity commanded it to be dry, and the dark earth appeared at his feet. Around him lofty trees spread their fruits to view; the pear, the pomegranate, and the apple, the green olive, and the luscious fig quivered before him, which, whenever he extended his hand to seize them, were snatched by the winds into clouds and obscurity."

"There, Tantalus, along the Stygian bound,
Pours out deep groans,—his groans through hell resound.
E'en in the circling flood refreshment craves
And pines with thirst amidst a sea of waves."

"... And of itself the water flies
All taste of living wight, as once it fled
The lip of Tantalus."
Milton.

Tartarus (Tar′tarus). An inner region of hell, to which the gods sent the exceptionally depraved.

Telchines (Telchi′nes). People of Rhodes, who were envious sorcerers and magicians.

Tellus (Tel′lus). A name of Cybele, wife of Saturn, and the Roman deity of mother-earth.

Tempests, see Fro.

Temple. An edifice erected to the honor of a god or goddess in which the sacrifices were offered.

Tenth Muse. Sappho was so called.

Tereus (Ter′eus) was a son of Mars. He married Procne, daughter of the king of Athens, but became enamored of her sister Philomela, who, however, resented his attentions, which so enraged him that he cut out her tongue. When Procne heard of her husband's unfaithfulness she took a terrible revenge (see Itys). Procne was turned into a swallow, Philomela into a nightingale, Itys into a pheasant, and Tereus into a hoopoe, a kind of vulture, some say an owl.

Tergemina (Tergemi′na). A name of Diana, alluding to her triform divinity as goddess of heaven, earth, and hell.

Terminus (Ter′minus). The Roman god of boundaries.

Terpsichore (Terpsich′ore). One of the nine Muses; she presided over dancing.

Terra. The Earth; one of the most ancient of the Grecian goddesses.

Thalestris (Thales′tris). A queen of the Amazons.

Thalia (Thali′a). One of the nine Muses; she presided over festivals, pastoral poetry and comedy.

Thalia (Thali′a). One of the Graces. (See Charities).

Thamyris (Tham′yris). A skilful singer, who presumed to challenge the Muses to sing, upon condition that if he did not sing best they might inflict any penalty they pleased. He was, of course, defeated, and the Muses made him blind.

Theia (The′ia) or Thea. A daughter of Uranus and Terra, wife of Hyperion.

Themis (The′mis), a daughter of Coelus and Terra, and wife of Jupiter, was the Roman goddess of laws, ceremonies, and oracles.

Theseus (The'seus). One of the most famous of the Greek heroes. He was a son of Aegeus, king of Athens. He rid Attica of Procrustes and other evil-doers, slew the Minotaur, conquered the Amazons and married their Queen.

"Breasts that with sympathizing ardor glowed,
And holy friendship such as Theseus vowed."
Budgell.

Thesmorphonis (Thesmorpho'nis). A name of Ceres.

Thetis (The'tis). A sea-goddess, daughter of Nereus and Doris. Her husband was Peleus, king of Thessaly, and she was the mother of the famous Achilles, whom she rendered all but invulnerable by dipping him into the River Styx. See Achilles.

Thief, see Laverna, Mercury.

Thor. The Scandinavian war-god (son of Odin), who had rule over the aerial regions, and, like Jupiter, hurled thunder against his foes.

Thor's Belt is a girdle which doubles his strength whenever the war-god puts it on.

Thoth. The Mercury of the Egyptians.

Thread of Life, see Fates.

Thunderbolts, see Cyclops.

Thunderer, The, Jupiter. See Tonitrualis.

"O king of gods and men, whose awful hand
Disperses thunder on the seas and land,
Disposing all with absolute command."
Virgil.

"The eternal Thunderer sat enthroned in gold."
Homer.

"So when thick clouds enwrap the mountain's head,
O'er heaven's expanse like one black ceiling spread;
Sudden the Thunderer, with flashing ray,
Bursts through the darkness and lets down the day."
Pope.

Thya (Thy′a), a name of Ops.
Thyades (Thya′des). Priestesses of Bacchus, who ran wild in the hills, wearing tiger-skins and carrying torches.
Thyrsus (Thyr′sus), a kind of javelin or staff carried by Dionysus and his attendants. It was usually wreathed with ivy and topped by a pine-cone. See Bacchus.
Tides, see Narayan.
Time (or Saturn). The husband of Virtue and father of Truth.
Tisiphone (Tis-iph′one). One of the Furies, daughter of Nox and Acheron, who was the minister of divine vengeance upon mankind.
Titan (Ti′tan). Elder brother of Saturn, who made war against him, and was ultimately vanquished by Jupiter.
Titans (Ti′tans) were the supporters of Titan in his war against Saturn and Jupiter. They were the sons of Uranus and Gaea, men of gigantic stature and of great strength. Hence our English word Titanic.
Tithonus (Ti-tho′nus). The husband of Aurora. At the request of his wife the gods granted him immortality, but she forgot at the same time to ask that he should be granted perpetual youth. The consequence was that Tithonus grew old and decrepit, while Aurora remained as fresh as the morning. The gods, however, changed him into a grasshopper, which is supposed to moult as it gets old, and grows young again.
Tityus (Tit′yus). A son of Jupiter. A giant who was thrown into the

innermost hell for insulting Diana. He, like Prometheus, has a vulture constantly feeding on his ever-growing liver, the liver being supposed to be the seat of the passions.

Toil, see Atlas.

Tombs, see Manes.

Tongue, see Tereus.

Tonitrualis (Tonitrua'lis), or Tonans. The Thunderer; a name of Jupiter.

Towers, see Cybele.

Tragedy, see Melpomene.

Trees, see Aristaeus.

Tribulation, see Echidna.

Triformis (Trifor'mis), see Tergemina.

Triptolemus (Triptol'emus). A son of Oceanus and Terra. He was a great favorite of the goddess Ceres, who cured him of a dangerous illness when he was young, and afterwards taught him agriculture. She gave him her chariot, which was drawn by dragons, in which he carried seed-corn to all the inhabitants of the earth, and communicated the knowledge given to him by Ceres. Cicero mentions a Triptolemus as the fourth judge of the dead.

"Triptolemus, whose useful cares intend
The common good."
Pope.

Triterica (Triteri'ca). Bacchanalian festivals.

Tritons (Tri'tons) were sons of Triton, a son of Neptune and Amphitrite. They were the trumpeters of the sea-gods, and were depicted as a sort of mermen—the upper half of the body being like a man, and the lower half like dolphins.

Trivia (Tri'via). A surname given to Diana, because she presided over all places where three roads meet.

Trophonius (Tropho'nius). A legendary hero of architecture, and one of Jupiter's most famous oracles.

Troy. The classic poets say that the walls of this famous city were built by the magic sound of Apollo's lyre. See Dardanus, Helen, Hercules, Paris.

Trumpeters, see Tritons.

Truth. A daughter of Time, because Truth is discovered in the course of Time. Democritus says that Truth lies hidden at the bottom of a well.

Tutelina (Tutel′ina). A rural divinity—the goddess of granaries.

Two Faces, see Janus.

Typhoeus (Typhoe′us), see Typhon.

Typhon (Ty′phon). A monster with a hundred heads who made war against the gods, but was crushed by Jove's thunderbolts, and imprisoned under Mount Etna.

"... Typhon huge, ending in snaky twine."
Milton.

Typhon (Ty′phon). In Egyptian mythology the god who tried to undo all the good work effected by Osiris. According to the Greek writer, Hesiod, Typhon or Typhoeus was a monster giant, son of Terra and Tartarus.

Uller (Ul′ler). The Scandinavian god who presided over archery and duels.

Ulysses (Ulys′ses). A noted king of Ithaca, whose exploits in connection with the Trojan war, and his adventures on his return therefrom, are the subject of Homer's Odyssey. His wife's name was Penelope, and he was so much endeared to her that he feigned madness to get himself excused from going to the Trojan war; but this artifice was discovered, and he was compelled to go. He was of great help to the Grecians, and forced Achilles from his retreat, and obtained the charmed arrows of Hercules from Philoctetes, and used them against the Trojans. He enabled Paris to shoot one of them at the heel of Achilles, and so kill that charmed warrior. During his

wanderings on his homeward voyage he was taken prisoner by the Cyclopes and escaped, after blinding Polyphemus, their chief. At Aeolia he obtained all the winds of heaven, and put them in a bag; but his companions, thinking that the bags contained treasure which they could rob him of when they got to Ithaca, cut the bags, and let out the winds, and the ships were immediately blown back to Aeolia. After Circe had turned his companions into swine on an island where he and they were shipwrecked, he compelled the goddess to restore them to their human shape again. As he passed the islands of the Sirens he escaped their allurements by stopping the ears of his companions with wax, and fastening himself to the mast of his ship. His wife Penelope was a pattern of constancy; for, though Ulysses was reported to be dead, she would not marry any one else, and had the satisfaction of finding her husband return after an absence of about twenty years. The Greek name of Ulysses is Odysseus.
"To show what pious wisdom's power can do,
The poet sets Ulysses in our view."

Undine (Un'dine). A water-nymph, or sylph, who, according to fable, might receive a human soul by marrying a mortal.
Unknown God, An. With reference to this God, nothing can be more appropriate than St. Paul's address to the Athenians, as recorded in the 17th chapter of the Acts of the Apostles:
"Ye men of Athens, I perceive that in all things ye are too superstitious. For as I passed by, and beheld your devotions, I found an altar with this inscription, TO THE UNKNOWN GOD. Whom therefore ye ignorantly worship, him declare I unto you. God that made the world and all things therein, seeing that he is Lord of heaven and earth, dwelleth not in temples made with hands; neither is worshiped with men's hands, as though he needed anything, seeing he giveth to all life, and breath, and all things; and hath made of one blood all nations of men for to dwell on all the face of the earth, and hath determined the times before appointed, and the bounds of

their habitation; that they should seek the Lord, if haply they might feel after him, and find him, though he be not far from every one of us: for in him we live, and move, and have our being; as certain also of your own poets have said, For we are also his offspring. Forasmuch then as we are the offspring of God, we ought not to think that the Godhead is like unto gold, or silver, or stone, graven by art and man's device. And the times of this ignorance God winked at; but now commandeth all men everywhere to repent: because he hath appointed a day, in the which he will judge the world in righteousness by that man whom he hath ordained; whereof he hath given assurance unto all men, in that he hath raised him from the dead."

Unxia (Unx'ia). A name of Juno, relating to her protection of newly married people.

Urania (Ura'nia). A daughter of Jupiter and Mnemosyne—one of the Muses who presided over astronomy.

Venus de Milo

Uranus (Ura'nus), literally, heaven. Son and husband of Gaea, the Earth, and father of Chronos (Time) and the Titans. The Greek name of Coelus; his descendants are sometimes called Uranides.

Urgus (Ur'gus). A name of Pluto, signifying the Impeller.

Ursa Major (Ur'sa Ma'jor), see Calisto.

Ursa Minor (Ur'sa Mi'nor), see Arcas.

Usurers, see Jani.

Utgard Loki (Ut'gard Lo'ki). In Scandinavian mythology the king of the giants.

Valhalla (Valhal'la). The Scandinavian temple of immortality, inhabited by the souls of heroes slain in battle.

Vali (Va'li). The Scandinavian god of archery.

Valleys, see Vallonia.

Vallonia (Vallo'nia). The goddess of valleys.

Varuna (Varu'na). The Hindoo Neptune—generally represented as a white man riding on a sea-horse, carrying a club in one hand and a rope or noose to bind offenders in the other.

Vedius (Ve'dius). The same as Vejovis.

Vejovis (Vejo'vis). "Little Jupiter"—a name given to Jupiter when he appeared without his thunder.

Vejupiter (Veju'piter), see Vejovis.

Vengeance, see Nemesis.

Venus (Ve'nus). The goddess of beauty, and mother of love. She is said to have sprung from the foam of the sea, and was immediately carried to the abode of the gods on Olympus, where they were all charmed with her extreme beauty. Vulcan married her, but she permitted the attentions of others of the gods, and notably of Mars, their offspring being Hermione, Cupid, and Anteros. After this she left Olympus and fell in love with Adonis, a beautiful youth, who was killed when hunting a wild boar. Venus indirectly caused the Trojan War, for, when the goddess of discord had thrown among the goddesses the golden apple inscribed "To the fairest," Paris adjudged the apple to Venus, and she inspired him with love for Helen, wife of Menelaus, king of Sparta. Paris carried off Helen to Troy, and the Greeks pursued and besieged the city (see Helen, Paris, and

Troy). Venus is mentioned by the classic poets under the names of Aphrodite, Cypria, Urania, Astarte, Paphia, Cythera, and the laughter-loving goddess. Her favorite residence was at Cyprus. Incense alone was usually offered on her altars, but if there was a victim it was a white goat. Her attendants were Cupids and the Graces.

Verticordia (Verti'cor'dia). A Roman name of Venus, signifying the power of love to change the hard-hearted. The corresponding Greek name was Epistrophia.

Vertumnus (Vertum'nus) ("the Turner," "Changer"). God of spring, or, as some mythologists say, of the seasons; the husband of Pomona, the goddess of fruits and orchards.

Vesta (Ves'ta), daughter of Saturn and Cybele, was the goddess of the hearth and its fire. She had under her special care and protection a famous statue of Minerva, before which the Vestal Virgins kept a fire or lamp constantly burning.

Vestal Virgins (Ves'tal Vir'gins) were the priestesses of Vesta, whose chief duty was to see that the sacred fire in the temple of Vesta was not extinguished. They were always selected from the best families, and were under a solemn vow of chastity, and compelled to live perfectly pure lives.

Vialis (Via'lis). A name of Mercury, because he presided over the making of roads.

Victory (Vic'tory). A goddess, the daughter of Styx and Acheron, generally represented as flying in the air holding out a wreath of laurel. Her Greek name is Nike (Nicē). See Nicephorus.

Vidor. A Scandinavian god, who could walk on the water and in the air. The god of silence (corresponding with the classic Harpocrates).

Virtue. A goddess worshiped by most of the ancients under various names. The way to the temple of honor was through the temple of virtue.

Virtuous Women, see Juno.

Vishnu (Vish'nu). The Preserver, the principal Hindoo goddess.

Volupia (Volu'pia), see Angeronia.

Vulcan (Vul'can), the god of fire, was the son of Jupiter and Juno. He offended Jupiter, and was by him thrown out of heaven; he was nine days falling, and at last dropped into Lemnos with such violence that he broke his leg, and was lame forever after. Vulcan was married to Venus. He is supposed to have formed Pandora out of clay. His servants were the Cyclopes. He was the patron deity of blacksmiths, and as the smelter or softener of metal bears also the name of Mulciber.

"Men call him Mulciber; and how he fell
From heaven, they fabled, thrown by angry Jove,
Sheer o'er the crystal battlements."
Milton.

Vulcanalia (Vulcān-al'ia) were Roman festivals in honor of Vulcan, at which the victims (certain fish and animals) were thrown into the fire and burned to death.
War, see Bellona, Chemos, Mars.
Water, see Canopus.
Water-Nymphs, see Doris.
Wax Tablets, see Calliope.
Wealth, see Cuvera.
Weaving, see Ergatis.
Weeding, see Runcina.
Weights and Measures, see Mercury.
Well, see Truth.
West Wind, see Favonius.
Winds, see Aurora, Auster, Boreas, Zephyr.
Wine, see Bacchus, Suradevi.
Wisdom, see Pollear, Minerva.
Woden (Wo'den), the Anglo-Saxon form of the Scandinavian god Odin; Wednesday is called after him.
Women's Safeguard, see Sospita.
Woodpecker, see Picus.
Woods, see Dryads.

World, see Chaos.

Xanthus (Xan´thus), the name of the wonderful horse of Achilles.

Yama (Ya´ma). The Hindoo devil, generally represented as a terrible monster of a green color, with flaming eyes.

Ygdrasil (Yg´dra´sil). The famous ash-tree of Scandinavian mythology, under which the gods held daily council.

Ymir (Y´mir). The Scandinavian god, corresponding to Chaos of the classics.

Youth (perpetual), see Tithonus.

Zephyr (Zeph´yr) or Zephyrus (Zeph´yrus). The west wind and god of flowers, a son of Astraeus and Aurora (Eos). See Favonius.

"Wanton Zephyr, come away.

.　.　.　.　.

The sun, and Mira's charming eyes,
At thy return more charming grow.
With double glory they appear,
To warm and grace the infant year."
John Hughes, 1700.

Zetes (Ze´tes), with his brother Calais, drove the Harpies from Thrace.

Zethus (Ze´thus), twin brother of Amphion. He was the son of Antiope and Zeus. See Amphion.

Zeus (Zūs). The Greek name of Jupiter, the greatest god in Grecian mythology. He was the god of the sky and its phenomena, and as such was worshiped on the highest mountains, on which he was enthroned. From Zeus come all changes in the sky or the winds; he is the gatherer of the clouds which dispense fertilizing rain; and is also the thunderer and hurler of lightning.